Spanish:

Learn Spanish for beginners the fun way: Spanish Grammar, pronunciation, reading and writing.

(+ Short Stories)

document

Contents

INTRODUCTION

Welcome to your introduction to Spanish! While English is without a doubt one of the most important languages in the world, Spanish is the second most learned by its native speakers, the top language being Mandarin.

Learning Spanish is not as difficult as it seems, assuming you've got the right guidance. However, there are certainly quite a few obstacle that more often than not will get in your way. Native speakers tend to speak very quickly, the Spanish way of pronouncing "r" is one that feels strange to native English speakers, and text, while it's fairly easy to read once you know the rules, can become tricky once you put syllable stressing into play.

Nonetheless, this book is here to help you with some grammar theory, along with some tips and tricks aimed to get you to get a hold into the world of words of all Hispanic speakers.

The first rule for this is to find your motivation for learning the language.

Numbers and communication are important but there's also a bit of beauty that comes from learning a foreign language. Getting to understand a language means not only you're closing a gap between you and someone who doesn't know how to communicate with you, it means giving a glance to their story and culture, how they came to be, how they think, and to get a better grasp of what they are now.

If that's not your thing, you may be interested on their media, which is great too! Translations are a great way to get a message delivered through TV or social media, yet nothing beats to get the very exact meaning of someone's wording, something that is inevitable to be lost in translation. Being the translator may also be profitable for you!

Whatever your motivation is, always keep it in mind and hold it close to your heart because the next step depends of this: You need to be dedicated.

Saying you want to do something is one thing but giving up or not after the first month is what makes the difference between learning nothing and speaking fluently.

At any time of your day you should dedicate at least an hour to study. Whether it's a refresher or a tackle into a subject you don't quite get, it's important for you to never give up out of boredom or frustration when learning Spanish or any other language. Recall what made you study in it the first place and make it your star, your horizon.

That being said, there are things we can focus on to make it easier for you to not give up. The first one being not get into the specifics of grammar too early. Try to get your focus first into reading and speaking before jumping into it.

If you feel like you are getting stuck at some point, you may want to leave them for later assuming they won't hinder your progress. Don't abandon them, just leave them for later when you feel you're getting used to it.

Get exposed to Spanish in whichever way you see fit. It doesn't matter if you don't get it, what matters is that your learning experience will feel more natural. Find some friends who actually speak Spanish and give your accent a try. Most likely both your accent and the structure of your message will be terrible but you'll get useful tips on how to fix your problems. If you don't know anyone, try to practice speaking to yourself out loud, give your best into sounding as natural as possible, maybe even get to know people online willing to practice with you.

If you follow these tips, you'll be able to communicate in Spanish before you know it. Of course, even taking all of this into account, there are still some pitfalls you still need to be wary of.

First of all, there are cognates, words that are very similar to one another between both languages. Spanish shares a lot of its vocabulary with English, more that you would expect, which is wonderful as it makes it a lot easier to learn. This comes with its own set of problems, though. There are also false cognates, also called "false friends", words that sounds the same as other words in English but aren't.

Just to name a few examples, we use the word "Translation" to refer to something being rewritten for an audience of a different language. This word sounds like "Translación", but this one refers to the movement of an object in space in geometry or a planet's orbit, usually Earth.

There's also the word "delight", which sounds a lot like "Delito". "Delight" refers to the feeling or action of taking pleasure of something. "Delito", on the other hand, means crime, felony, or misdeed.

This is why, even if you are almost positive something have certain meaning, it is highly recommended to have a dictionary at hand to check if that's true. This way you can avoid misunderstandings or offending people by accident.

It is also highly advise to keep in mind the region you want to communicate with when learning Spanish. Despite many Hispanic countries being neighbors, lots of their words mean something completely different, specially when using vulgar words making reference to sex.

Take for example the word "arrecho". It is mostly used as a vulgar adjective but the properties it gives to its noun vary a lot depending on the country. In Venezuela, Honduras and Nicaragua, it's a slang that means being irritated, furious, even choleric; it may also describe a person as exceptionally daredevil or hardworking. In Panama, Argentina, and Uruguay, however, it is use to describe a person as aroused or easy to arouse.

Learning a language is a work of love, it takes dedication to make it bloom into its fullest and there are plenty of sharp thorn along the way. However, if you remind yourself of your goals, give it enough time, and get the right tools, little by little you'll master this language so full of emotions and beauty.

Cómo leer en español (HOW TO READ IN SPANISH):

In English, writing can be a nightmare. Because of how different spoken English is compared to its written counterpart, competitions based on spelling called "Spelling Bees" are pretty much mandatory to make kids and even adults take more interest on this necessary part of their language. There's even a "welcome to English" joke where it's explained in detail how "Goathy" can be pronounced as fish!

Spanish, however, doesn't have any of this problems. Why? Because Spanish has a phonetic written language, which means everything sounds exactly as it is written (most of the time). There are still a handful of rules to remember, but once you get the hang of them, there's no way you're getting anything confused. You won't be left wondering if you should spell the "l" in "Almond" or something like that. "Almendra" will always sound the same everywhere you read it, unless local accent happens.

Los sonidos del Español (SPANISH SOUNDS):

English, despite having only 5 written vowels, has around 12 different vowel sounds used depending on the combination of letters used, without counting diphthongs. Spanish has the same 5 vowels, but limits itself to give those 5 vowels a sound. Their pronunciation is as follows:

A — Like "a" in "father"
E — Like "e" in "egg" or "leg
I — Like "ee" in "meet" and "beet"
O — Similar to the "o" in "open" and "phone", except the short "u" sound at the end is omitted
U — Like "oo" in "boot" or "loot"

English has a tendency of omitting as many sounds as it can. If a syllable is stressed, only the vowels on that syllable are pronounced on their plenitude. This is why words like "shaking" and "bacon" can rhyme in English, "king" and "con" lose all the stress on their vowel and end up sounding similar.

This can't happen in Spanish. Stressing rules and weak vowels still exist in this language but an unstressed sound never distorts enough to sound similar to another sound. All I's sound like other I's and all O's sound like other O's.

Take for example Rama and Ramo. Assuming both words had their "Ra" stressed in English, both words would sound similar to Ramuh. In Spanish, Rama sounds like "Ram-ah" and Ramo like "Ram-oh", as suggested by the guide above.

The consonants are very similar as they are in English, with a few exceptions. Their sounds are as explained below:

B: As in the "b" in "ball", "balloon", and "bun".
D: As in the "d" in "dog", "doll", and "dome".
F: As in the "f" in "fierce", "fang", and "fight"
H: It's completely silent. See explanation below
J: As in the "h" in "hot", "ham", and "heist"
K: As in the "k" in "key", "kilogram", and "kill"
L: As in the "l" in "life", "laugh", and "like"
M: As in the "m" in "monkey", "money", and "man"
N: As in the "n" in "nature, "nasty", and "nice"
P: As in the "p" in "power", "paste", and "plum"
S: As in the "s" in "side", "seize", and "sentient"
T: As in the "t" in "tick", take", and "tact"
V: As in the "v" in "vague", "vain", and "vinyl"
W: As in the "w" in "winter", "winner", and "wing". This letter has no words with origin in Spanish
X: As in the "xc" in "excess", "exciting", and "exception"
Y: As in the "y" in "yacht", "yeast", and "yes". If it doesn't have a vowel in front of it or is on its own, its sound becomes as if it's the vowel "I"
Z: As in the "z" in "zoo", "zone", and "zany"

While Spanish doesn't vary the sound of its letter from word to word, there are still some cases in which position and combinations of some of them will cause their sound to change, which lead us to the more complicated sounds of the alphabet.

C sounds like the Spanish S when accompanied by the vowels E and I, otherwise it sounds like the Spanish K. When an H is next to it, they merge into a new consonant, Ch. Spanish Ch sounds like the "ch" on "chill", "chamber", or "chief".

G sounds similar to the "g" in "go", "god", and "goose" except when accompanied by the vowels E and I, in which case it sounds like Spanish J. To get a sound as in "go" with I and E, U is placed between G and either vowel. In those cases, the U turns silent and the sound becomes as in "gill" and "get".

While the Spanish B and V sound different enough they're their own letters, some countries don't see them as such. For most Latinamerican countries the Spanish V sounds the same exact way as its B partner. Spanish S and Z have the same problem, Z loses its vibrations and becomes a S sound.

The letter Ñ is also a tricky one for English speakers, since it doesn't exist in English at all. To pronounce it, we make a sound similar to the "ny" in "pinyon" or "canyon". If we want to write "ñ" without having to look up a word with that letter every time, we can use Alt Codes to get it. By holding Alt on your keyboard, typing 164, and letting Alt go, you'll get "ñ". You can get capital "Ñ"s if you type 165 instead.

You can also configure your keyboard to have an Hispanic layout by configuring your Operative System, Ñ should be on L's right, but this will modify on its entirety the layout of your symbols as well. Don't use this option unless you know how to switch back and forth between keyboard layouts.

Back to letters, the Spanish Q is an interesting one. On its native use, it's only ever accompanied by E and I with an U in the middle of the two, and sounds like the Spanish K even without the U or using any other letter. However, this only happens with words imported from outside Spanish.

The Spanish L changes its sound completely when in company of another L. When it becomes LL, it sounds like the Spanish Y, except it sounds like a single L when it doesn't have a vowel, this last doesn't happen in Spanish, though.

Lastly, we have the Spanish R, the sound most Spanish learners struggle with. This language has two kinds of R: When the letter R is at the start of a word or together with another R, it makes the sound RR (Double R) instead. Otherwise, it's just a single R.

Most people will tell you Single R sounds very similar to the English D. This is mostly true, but you have to make sure the sound made is quick and weak, as if you barely want to be aware that sound exist. A soft flap of your tongue behind your upper teeth should be enough, as if when pronouncing the "tt" in "butter".

Double R is the more complicated one, as it doesn't have an equivalent in English. To make this sound, hold the tip of your tongue behind your teeth as if you were to make the Spanish R, hold it there, and pass air right behind it. The result should be a repeating vibrating sound similar to snoring or a cat's purring.

You probably won't get this last sound on your first try. This is normal, many English Speakers trying to learn Spanish have problem with this, there's no need to worry, come back later and keep practicing until you get it right. Take it as if you're practicing whistling.

As mentioned before, there are vowels with strong and weak vowel sounds just like many languages, but all of them are pronounced out loud if written, not a single letter is muted unless some other rule says otherwise. There are only three cases in which a letter becomes silent. Those are:

H: This letter is always silent unless combined with "C", which creates a new consonant, "Ch".

U: It becomes silent if it's placed right after "G" or "Q" but only before "E" and "I".

Ps: If it's at the very start of the word, the P behind S becomes silent, otherwise all the letters are pronounce.

EXERSICES:

Read and repeat out loud the word presented to you. Try to mimic the sound made to the best of your capabilities.

Group 1: Letters
A — E — I — O — U — Be — Ce — De — Efe — Ge — Ache — Jota — Ca — Ele — Eme — Ene — Eñe — Pe — Cu — Erre — Ese — Te — Ve — Equis — Ye — Zeta

Group 2: Short simple words
Mana — Papa — Mapa — Casa — Lata — Pata — Gata — Pepe — Meme — Vete — Tina — Lila — Lili — Mini — Tomo — Loro — Polo — Momo — Mono — Foto — Dodo — Como — Gurú — Puro — Muro — Duro — Suda — Uno — Jugo — Luto — Ludo — Uni — Mute

Group 3: Short words with compound consonants
Plata — Manta — Menta — Piensa — Miente — Crear — Preso — Prestar — Sentir — Plan — Hervir — Norte — Riesgo — Prisa — Trigo — Prisma — Fresco — Cromo — Concha — Presa — Bruma — Grecia — Fregar — Claro — Frito — Petro — Frasco — Grieta — Grumo — Tropas

Grupo 4: Longer words
Marino — Demencia — Territorio — Gracioso — Maestro — Ministerio — Granjero — Moneda — Pensionado — Depositar — Comida — Alcachofa — Paralelo — Pajarera — Comunicado — Experiencia — Papeleo — Pelota — Plastilina — Remoto — Afilado — Computadora — Cableado — Marcador — Sacapuntas — Borrador — Cargador — Transmitir — Comodidad — Seriedad

Grupo 5: Words with many R sounds, RR sounds, and Ñ sounds

Ñame — Maña — Recreo — Correa — Caño — Champiñón — Añorar — Año — Roñoso — Lagaña — Ñoño — Piraña — Maraña — Araña — Alimaña — Patrañas — Ronrronear — Ñandú — Hazaña — Moño — Acuñar — Caña — Arremeter — Carrara — Acarrear — Carrucha — Compañía — Daño — Enseñar — Cañón — Desempeño — Pîña — Uña — Dueño — Añadir — Reseña — Ceño — Puñal — Engañar — Montaña — Mañana — Pequeño — Señuelo — Puño — Extrañar — Campaña — Niño — Diseño — Español — Baño — Paño — Antaño — Riñón — Entrañar — Extrañar — Señal — Añadir — Cariño — Pañal — Rebaño — Cuñado — Otoño

Acento y acentuación de palabras (STRESS AND WORD STRESSING):

Both English and Spanish have the concept of Stressing or Word Stressing. This makes it so some syllables in a word have an stronger sound than others. In English, this is used to differentiate words that might sound similar but are very different.

In Spanish we use them for the same purpose but it is grammatically shown on texts of that language. To give an accent to a word, we place a tiny slash over the vowel called tilde, which looks like a tiny 45 degrees slash above the vowel.

It is very important to keep stressing rules in mind . While Hottle and Hotel looks completely different in paper but sound similar in English, a mistake like that in Spanish could lead to a confusion similar to English's Desert, which can be either an arid biome or a light meal after eating.

One particular infamous word for this is "papa". Without an accent, it means potato. But when given an accent at the last syllable it becomes "papá", which means dad. Another less mentioned possibility but just as bad is the chance of confusing two completely different verb tenses.

This can become a confusing topic for English speakers, so it is recommended to approach it with patience. If you feel like you don't get it, come back later after you feel you've become a little more familiar with the language.

Reglas de Acentuación (STRESSING RULE.

All words have a single syllable stressed but not all words have their stress marked by a tilde, unmarked stressing is called "prosodic stress". To know what words we should stress in paper and what words we should not we use the following rules:

All words made out of a single vowel have prosodic stress unless a diacritic tilde is needed. Diacritic tilde is still too advance so it will be touched with care later.

Words with their stress on their last syllable are grammatically stressed only when they end on any vowel, -n, and -s

Volver**á** — Caf**é** — Manat**í** — Vol**vió** — Tabl**ón** — Qui**zás**
Cor**al** — Can**tor** — Soli**dez** — Amis**tad**

Words with their stress on their second to last syllable are grammatically stressed only when they end on a consonant that isn't -n or -s

Árbol — **Lá**piz — **Ál**bum — **Út**il
Pape**ler**a — Des**lic**e — Des**tin**o — **Pin**ten — **Pis**tas

All words stressed on their third to last syllable and below are always grammatically stressed

Cándido — **Rá**pido — **Fí**sica — Mate**má**tica — **Á**guila — **Dé**cimo

In the case of a diphthong, the vowel of a syllable is a

compound of multiple vowels. A diphthongs in Spanish only happens when a strong vowel (A, E, or O) is paired with weak vowels (I and U). Strong vowels paired with other strong vowels or stressed weak vowels can't form a diphthong, but two weak vowel can unless its paired with a copy of itself. If the diphthong isn't broken by stressing, it follows the previously mentioned stressing rules.

Disposi**ción** — A**pré**cias — **Béis**bol
Pre**sa**gio — Poten**cia** — **Fies**ta

If a syllable that could be a diphthong on normal circumstances separates its vowels into different syllables because of stressing, that stressing takes priority and is marked grammatically, even if it doesn't follow the previously mentioned rules.

Ma**íz** — **Crí**a — Cafe**í**na — San**dí**a

All composite words, words created by combining two other words, follow the previously mention rules except for words compounded with -mente. In those cases, stressing rules are followed as if the word didn't have -mente attached to it.

Cienpi**és** — Porta**lám**paras — Hazmerre**ír** — Rompecolch**ón**
Cuenta**go**tas — Cumplea**ños** — Afrodecen**dien**te — Matamos**qui**tos
Velo**z**mente — Cien**tí**ficamente — Hipo**té**ticamente — **Fá**cilmente

EXCERSICES:

Using the stressing rules given above, put a tilde into the following words.

Personas	Caliente	Maquina	Mente	Arido	Anestesia
Compresion	Corazon	Estupidez	Camello	Arlequin	Desden
Antiestres	Parodia	Analisis	Sentido	Manantial	Concierto
Fantastico	Magico	Siniestro	Sadico	Sorpresa	Inusual
Intensamente	Mania	Pelicula	Tijeras	Manoslibres	Cirugia
Novato	Pesimo	Parasito	Pescado	Camarote	Epico
Sospecha	Aroma	Alcohol	Proposito	Pension	Agua
Hibrido	Llano	Mansion	Gemir	Indigena	Audaz
Friamente	Inmundo	Solteria	Banda	Sonico	Estelar
Intrepido	Basico	Comodidad	Amor	Cienpies	Donacion
Insensato	Plata	Anillo	Moneda	Amplio	Astrologia
Aparecia	Flor	Pancreas	Criar	Sencillo	Crio
Jerarquia	Memoria	Predecible	Paralelo	Indecencia	Poster
Cumpleaños	Espacio	Correo	Numero	Porcentaje	Corriente

SUSTANTIVOS (NOUN):

Nouns take the role of the object that do the action of the verb in a sentence. We usually use them to represent people, animals, or actual objects. They can also be used to refer to abstract concepts like love, time, and war.

Nouns are word that define what we are talking about on the sentence. They are words that bring information about themselves just by being there. They can't be simple words like "I", "You", or "Me", words that target a person instead of mentioning them are called pronouns.

These are pronouns:
Ellos están ocupados — They are busy
Nosotros estamos en problemas — We are in trouble
Yo como poco en la cena — I eat little on dinner

These are actual nouns:
La empresa es exitosa alrededor del mundo — The company is successful around the world
Rodrigo recoge la basura del parque — Rodrigo picks up the trash at the park
Gabriel hace su tarea de mañana — Gabriel is doing tomorrow's homework

Sustantivos contables e incontables (COUNTABLE AND NON-COUNTABLE NOUNS):

Just like English, Spanish classifies their nouns as countable and non-countable. However, there's a huge difference on how those types or nouns are seen in Spanish.

If you are not familiar with this concept or don't remember it very well, countable nouns are those which we can tell how many of something are on a group by using only numbers. In this group we include animals, materials represented on units of measure, distinct objects, monetary units, among other things.

Perros (dogs), clavos (nails), discos (disks), uñas (fingernails), controles (controlers), archivos (archives), botones (buttoms), galletas (cookies), lazos (ribbons), ratones (mice), botellas (bottles).

Non-countables are those which we can't count without using units of measure like kilograms, seconds, litters, or grams. To give a few examples, water is non-countable, but litters and ounces of water are. Time itself is also non-countable, but we can count it on units like seconds, minutes, hours, weeks, and so on. Money is also non-countable, we can't measure money itself but we can count money using currency like dollars, euros, or pesos. We also include resources too tiny to reasonably consider countable and materials into this category.

Aceite (oil), vapor (steam), queso (cheese), plata (silver), arroz (rice), ropa (clothing), madera (wood), azucar (sugar), granito (granite), arena (sand), petróleo (petroleum), lechuga (lettuce).

Non-countables that turn into non-countable by adding units of measure:

Una taza de aceite (a cup of oil), un litro de agua (a litter of water), una cucharada de sal (a spoonful of salt), una rebanada de queso (a slice of cheese), un gramo de plata (a gram of silver), una hoja de lechuga (a leaf of lettuve), un barril de petróleo (a barrel of petroleum), un dolar (a dolar).

While the difference does exists and it shows grammatically, most Hispanic speakers do not realize they are talking about a countable or non-countable noun. This rarely comes into play since it's only used on quantity questions and exclamations. Also, Spanish speakers use the same word, "Cuanto", to talk about both "how much" and "how many".

Género del Sustantivo (NOUN GENDER):

Unlike English and similar to German, all nouns are referred to them as either masculine or feminine, usually represented by the "el" and "la" pronouns (Pronombre) respectively before the the word.

When referring to nouns which can vary their gender like "el niño" or "la niña" (kid), "el juez" or "la jueza" (judge), and "el abogado" o "la abogada" (lawyer); their gender is determined by the last letter on the word. Nouns ending with -o are masculine and words ending with -a are feminine.

Inanimate objects, abstract concepts and groups of people also have gender but it's purely grammatical and doesn't vary. There are also nouns that make mention of an either male or female individual. To determine those, we have to take a look at the following rules:

Sustantivo Masculino (MASCULINE NOUN):

Masculine nouns end their words with either -s, -n, -o, -r, -e, or -l. Most greek words with their word termination -ma, -pa, and -ta are also considered masculine nouns.

El montón, el cartón, el portón, el bien, el tragón, el botellón, el sifón, el trombón, el colchón.

El tormento, el conocimiento, el asiento, el reto, el momento, el boleto, el caldero, el dibujo.

El monitor, el proveedor, el ardor, el creador, el pastor, el rigor, el pensador, el calor.

El parque, el arranque, el cantante, el comandante, el fabricante, el paciente, el continente.

El panel, el cincel, el mal, el final, el grial, el hotel, el metal, el misil, el mentol, el local.

El poema, el drama, el problema, el idioma, el lema, el sistema, el dilema, el fonema.

El protagonista, el atleta, el deportista, el planeta, el astronauta, el ciclista, el atletista.

El mapa, el papa.

Days of the week (lunes [Monday], martes [Tuesday], miércoles [Wednesday], jueves [Thursday], viernes [Friday], sábado [Saturday] y domingo [Monday]) are also considered masculine nouns.

Lastly, compound nouns, words made out of multiple words like "cumpleaños" (birthday) are also masculine nouns.

El Lavamanos, el pisapapeles, el cuentagotas, el rompemuelas, el matasanos, el buscapersonas.

Spanish has plenty of exception placed there for the sake of giving harmony to the speech. There are some words that would be expected to be masculine but are in reality feminine, some examples are:

La fuente, la imagen, la nube, la cima, la dama, la trama, la tarde.

Sustantivos Femeninos (FEMININE NOUNS):

As mentioned before, feminine nouns are those with -a as their word termination. They can also end with -umbre, -ie, -ión, -dad, -tad or -is.

La jaula, la tregua, la ciencia, la jungla, la meta, la pereza, la grandeza, la moneda, la puerta.
La cumbre, la incertidumbre, la podredumbre, la costumbre, la servidumbre, la mansedumbre.
La especie, la serie, la efigie, la canicie, la burricie, la barbarie, la calvicie, la planicie, la coluvie.
La decisión, la acción, la posición, la comunicación, la mansión, la propoción, la precipitación.
La lealtad, la frialdad, la edad, la seriedad, la comunidad, la obscenidad, la oportunidad, la crueldad.
La parálisis, la crisis, la metástasis, la dosis, la tesis, la cirrosis, la prótesis, la síntesis, la mitósis.

When it comes to grammatical gender, words ending on -ión take priority over words ending just on -n.

La comunión, la aceptación, la colaboración, la alteración, la manifestación, la contención, la lesión.
El mentón, el vaivén, el alien, el abdomen, el afán, el festín, el cojín, el bombón, el jardín, el botín.

Words that follow the previous rules but start with a stressed a- or -ha are feminine nouns but are mentioned as masculine nouns when in singular. In plural, however, they are expressed as feminine nouns. Most common examples of this are "él agua" (water) and "el aguila" (eagle).

These rules cover most words in Spanish. However, as with any language, all rules have their own share of exceptions. Some exceptions to the previously mentioned rules are:

El día, el avión, el análisis, el énfasis, el éstasis, el camión, el puente, el pie.

Género de los animales (ANIMAL GENDER):

As to be expected, animals have gender distinctions too when it comes to grammar. They follow the same rules mentioned above, but there's are some details to keep in mind when mentioning animals.

Pets and sometimes livestock normally have their gender associated to the actual gender of the animal, as in "el perro" or "la perra" (dog), and "el gato" o "la gata" (cat). This usually doesn't include farm animals, since most of them have a name assigned to the specific gender of the specie, like bulls (los toros) and cows (las vacas) or some wild animals which have distinctive feautres between males and females.

Some examples of animals of distinct gender are:

Lion, lioness — León, leona
Rabbit — Conejo, coneja
Rooster, hen — Gallo, gallina
Buffalo — Búfalo, búfala
Camel — Camello, camella
Pig, sow — Cerdo, cerda
Wolf — Lobo, loba
Ram, sheep — Carnero, oveja
Goose — Ganso, gansa

A word of caution!: "Perra" can be considered an offensive slang for women. Spanish doesn't have a word of common use that differentiate between household female dogs and female dogs only used for breeding. There's nothing wrong in calling a female dog "perra", calling a woman "perra" will get you in trouble, though. Be very careful with this.

On the other hand, wild animals have their grammatical gender being the one given by their grammatical rules.

Ox — El buey
Squirrel — La ardilla
Whale — La ballena
Owl — El buho
Snail — El caracol
Eagle — El águila
Slug — La babosa

In case we want to mention an member of the specie that is of an specific gender we add to the right of the noun the adjectives "macho" and "hembra", which mean "male" and "female" respectively. The grammatical gender of the noun stays the same.

El avestruz macho — Male ostrich
La serpiente macho — Male snake
El caimán hembra — Female caiman
La rata hembra — Female rat

EXERSICES:

Get a pen and a piece of paper and pay attention to the following nouns, count how many of them are either masculine or feminine.

Group 1: Nouns with their article.

La cabeza — El arrecife — El profesor — La academia — El estudiante — El borrador — El pincel — El comedor — La madre — El padre — La nariz — El ojo — La cama — El árbol — El disco — El agua — El pretexto — La cumbre — La recepción — La moneda

29

— La colina — El caudal — La raiz — El pantano — El enano — La amistad — La nevera — El pollo — La gallina — La yegua — El pasto — La hierba — La colonia — El sabor — La punta — La aguja — La doctrina — La devoción — La puntería — El potencial — La humanidad — La caricia — La novedad

Group 2: Nouns without their article.

Drama — Retrato — Calzado — Media — Paciencia — Incertidumbre — Envidia — Orgullo — Cólera — Manuscrito — Dama — Caballero — Piedad — Arrogancia — Guerra — Crudeza — Renovación — Pérdida — Malentendido — Color — Baldosas — Llaves — Falda — Trenza — Sofá — Periódico — Pesadez — Comodidad — Deseo — Plato — Cuchillo — Servilleta — Distracción — Moneda — Billete — Podredumbre — Basura — Manifestación — Manera — Postura — Olla — Fuego — Horno — Cable — Página — Monitor — Botella — Pelota

Look at the following nouns and give them the preposition 'el' or 'la' depending if they're masculine or feminine respectively.

___ periódico	___ pesadez	___ comodidad	___ deseo	___ plato	___ tenedor
___ cuchillo	___ servilleta	___ distracción	___ moneda	___ billete	___ depósito
___ podredumbre	___ basura	___ manifestación	___ manera	___ postura	___ pena
___ olla	___ fuego	___ horno	___ cable	___ página	___ micrófono
___ monitor	___ botella	___ pelota	___ pulgar	___ lengua	___ leche
___ risa	___ puño	___ celebración	___ baya	___ máscara	___ músculo
___ flecha	___ cerveza	___ vino	___ soldado	___ enfermera	___ profesora
___ medalla	___ trofeo	___ piano	___ guitarra	___ bajo	___ trompeta
___ blanco	___ dardo	___ manzana	___ banana	___ mango	___ uva
___ cereza	___ ají	___ pan	___ dona	___ mazorca	___ maní
___ zanahoria	___ tomate	___ lechuga	___ coco	___ durazno	___ limón
___ berenjena	___ papa	___ kiwi	___ sartén	___ arroz	___ galleta
___ pez	___ pastel	___ helado	___ paleta	___ chocolate	___ pimienta
___ moto	___ automóvil	___ yate	___ bote	___ barco	___ cohete
___ satélite	___ ancla	___ paraguas	___ volcán	___ montaña	___ hospital
___ librería	___ estación	___ diamante	___ oro	___ plata	___ platino
___ martillo	___ ladrillo	___ pastilla	___ esponja	___ jabón	___ timbre
___ bacteria	___ lazo	___ globo	___ carta	___ lupa	___ candado

Adjectivos (ADJECTIVES):

Adjectives are words used to classify, describe, qualify or give attributes to a noun. They're used to give nouns more detail.

El agua caliente — Hot water
El hombre perezoso — Lazy man

Mentioning "agua" as it is is fine, but we can be more specific and make notice only of "el agua caliente". The same happens with "el hombre perezoso", without "peresozo", the lazy man is just no longer lazy, is just "el hombre".

Adjetivos antes o después del Sustantivo (ADJECTIVES BEFORE OR AFTER THE NOUN):

Since the adjective modifies the noun, they must go next to the noun. However, now the question is: On which side of the noun?

Adjectives can go either before or after the noun without making much of a difference. referring to old chair as "silla vieja" or "vieja silla" delivers almost the same message. Specifically, relative adjective can go anywhere after or before. These kind of adjectives possess two opposite extreme values which are relative to the perspective of the individual.

Frío/Caliente — Hot/Cold
Duro/Suave — Hard/Soft
Limpio/Sucio — Clean/Dirty
Fuerte/Débil — Strong/Weak
Alto/Bajo — Tall/Short
Pesado/Ligero — Heavy/Light
Brillante/Opaco — Shiny/Opaque
Sabio/Tonto — Wise/Fool
Claro/Oscuro — Light/Dark

However, placing an adjective after the noun points an important difference or distinction, while putting before the noun just names a characteristic of the object. While referring to "soft pillows", we can point out the pillow is soft by calling it "suave almohada", or identify a pillow that is remarkably soft by calling it "almohada suave".

Because of this, the most common order of adjective on free form language is Noun Adjective, the opposite is mostly used on literature.

There are nouns that can only be used either after or before the noun. Adjectives regarding color, shape, state and origin.

El vaso rojo — Red glass.
La casa amarilla — Yellow house
La uva morada — Purple grape
El café negro — Black coffee

El plato redondo — Round plate.
La pescera cuadrada — Squared fishbowl
La mesa triangular — Triangular table
El huevo ovalado — Oval egg

El recipiente vacío — Empty container
El plato lleno — Full plate [Serving of food]
El tornillo roto — Broken bolt
La caja abierta — Open box

La comunidad internacional — International community
La casa escocesa — Scottish household
La colonia espacial — Space colony
La cultura británica — Brittish culture

Also, numeral adjectives can go either after or before the noun, depending on the number and purpose. Cardinal adjectives always go before the noun when expressing a determined amount of that noun. Numeral adjectives can only be used on countable nouns, non-countable nouns must be turned into countable units first.

Una moneda — One coin
Dos pelotas — Two balls
Tres cabellos — Three hairs
Cuatro caramelos — Four taffies
Cinco camellos — Five camels

Diez kilos de azucar — Ten kilograms of sugar
Cien palomas — One hundred pigeons
Cincuenta y dos cartas — Fifty two cards

On the other hand, putting a cardinal adjective after the noun will let us know that a singular object has been tagged with a numeral as a way to identify it from the rest of the nouns similar to it, like cattle, experiments, or members of a group.

Agente doce — Agent Twelve
Vaca Mil setenta y nueve — Cow n° one thousand seventy nine
Experimento veintiséis — Experiment twenty six

We can use Ordinal adjectives before or after the noun to express a specific item inside of a sequence. Note that this is different from items tagged inside of a group, as tagging works only as identification. Sequences, on top of tagging, also follow a strict written pattern or sequence of objects one after another.

Keep in mind that, whenever we place a numeral ordinal adjective before a singular masculine noun and that adjective is "primero" (first) and "tercero" (third), their termination -o mutes and they become "primer" and "tercer" respectively. This change is known as an Apocope and we'll see it happen often.

Primera dama — First lady
Primer lugar — First place
Segunda Oportunidad — Second Chance
Tercera vuelta — Third lap
Tercer candidato — Third candidate
Última parada — Last Stop
Cuarto capítulo/Capítulo Cuatro — Forth Chapter/Chapter Four

Adjetivos Numerales (NUMERAL ADJECTIVES):

Numeral adjectives are those responsible of handling numbers on the sentence. They can be classified as cardinal, ordinal, multiplicative, and partitive.

Cardinal adjectives are numbers without any kind of grammatical modification. They are used to set a specific quantity of a specific noun.

Ordinal adjectives are used to give the idea of a numerical sequence being present on nouns such as floors, chapters, or places on a competition.

Multiplicative adjectives are used to point out a certain noun surpasses an object at something by an certain amount. They are most likely to be found in comparison and mentions of a streak. Normally only numbers involving doubles, triples and centuples are used.

Lastly, partitive nouns are the opposite of multiplicative nouns. They express they are a number of times smaller than another unit. They express fractions, rather than multiplication.

EXERSICES:

Repeat out loud the following cardinal numbers. It is recommended you write them as letters or repeat this as practice.

Group 1: Numbers from 1 to 10
Uno — One
Dos — Two
Tres — Three

Cuatro — Four
Cinco — Five
Seis — Six
Siete — Seven
Ocho — Eight
Nueve — Nine
Diez — Ten

Group 2: Numbers from 11 to 20
Once — Eleven
Doce — Twelve
Trece — Thriteen
Catorce — Fourteen
Qunice — Fifteen
Dieciseis — Sixteen
Diecisiete — Seventeen
Dieciocho — Eighteen
Diecinueve — Nineteen
Veinte — Twenty

Group 3: Numbers from 21 to 100
Veintiuno — Twenty one
Veintidos — Twenty two
Treinta — Thirty
Treinta y uno — Thirty one
Treinta y dos — Thrity two
Treinta y tres — Thirty three
Cuarenta y cuatro — Forty four
Cincuenta y cinco — Fifty five
Sesenta y seis — Sixty six
Setenta y siete — Seventy seven
Ochenta y ocho — Eighty eight
Noventa y nueve — Ninety nine

Group 4: Numbers from 101 to 999.999.999

Ciento uno — One hundred one

Ciento once — One hundred eleven

Doscientos veintidos — Two hundred twenty two

Trescientos treinta y tres — Three hundred thirty three

Mil — One thousand

Mil ciento once — One thousand one hundred eleven

Dos mil — Two thousand

Tres mil — Three thousand

Diez mil — Ten thousand

Cien mil — One hundred thousand

Un millón — One million

Once millones ciento once mil ciento once — Eleven million one hundred eleven thousand one hundred eleven

Novecientos noventa y nueve millones novecientos noventa y nueve mil novecientos noventa y nueve — Nine hundred ninety nine million nine hundred ninety nine thousand nine hundred and ninety nine.

EXERSICES:

Read the following Ordinal numbers and repeat them out loud, writing them is recommended. We'll only be learning the first 21 places, since anything above that is extremely rare to be mentioned in a casual conversation.

Primero — First

Segundo — Second

Tercero — Third

Cuarto — Fourth

Quinto — Fifth

Sexto — Sixth

Séptimo — Seventh

Octavo — Eighth
Noveno — Nineth
Décimo — Tenth
Undécimo — Eleventh
Duodécimo — Twelfth
Decimotercero — Thirteenth
Decimocuarto — Fourtheenth
Decimoquinto — Fifteenth
Decimosexto — Sixteenth
Decimoséptimo — Seventeenth
Decimoctavo — Eighteenth
Decimonoveno — Nineteenth
Vigésimo — Twentieth
Vigésimoprimero — Twenty-first

Write the following numbers written in Spanish into digits

Diez millones novecientos cuarenta y un mil trescientos veintidós 10.941.322	Mil millones treinta y nueve 1.000.000.039
Dos	Trece
Siete	Uno
Cinco	Nueve
Catorce	Doce
Quince	Diecinueve
Seis	Once
Diez	Diecisiete

Veinte	Treinta
Cuarenta y uno	Veintidos
Noventa y nueve	Sesenta y uno
Ochenta y tres	Cien
Ciento once	Ciento cincuenta
Doscientos quince	Trescientos noventa
Seiscientos cincuenta y cuatro	Novecientos once
Mil dos	Dos mil veinticuatro
Nueve mil uno	Tres mil doescientos diecinueve
Dieciseis mil setecientos sesenta	Treinta mil trescientos treinta y dos
Ciento noventa mil ochenta y uno	Quinientos mil doscientos
Seiscientos nueve	Ochocientos cuarenta y cuatro
Novecientos noventa	Setecientos trece
Mill diez	Cuatro mil cuatrocientos veintiocho
Seis mil once	Diez mil ciento uno
Ciento setenta y siete mil trece	Ciento veinticinco mil ciento treinta y ocho

Novecientos noventa y ocho mil doscientos	Quinientos cincuenta y un mil doscientos nueve

Un millón seiscientos dos mil ciento quince

Cuatro millones cuatrocientos cuarenta

Diez millones trescientos mil novecientos uno

Catorce millones noventa y nueve

Ciento veintitrés millones cuatrocientos cincuenta y seis mil setecientos ochenta y nueve

Novecientos millones novecientos mill novecientos noventa y nueve

Trescientos setenta y ocho millones quinientos setenta y un mil novecientos veinticuatro

Seiscientos treinta y seis millones novecientos dieciséis mi seiscientos veintinueve

Ochocientos noventa y seis millones setecientos treinta y dos mil noventa y tres

Seicientos trece millones ochocientos ochenta y dos mil cuatrocientos cincuenta y dos

Quinientos treinta y ocho millones seiscientos doce mil quinientos dieciséis

Doscientos un millones quinientos cincuenta mil seiscientos ochenta

Quinientos noventa y tres millones trescientos treinta y siete mil novecientos cuarenta y cuatro

Ochocientos veintisiete millones novecientos diez mil trescientos sesenta y ocho

Cuatrocientos noventa y dos millones novecientos cuarenta y cuatro mil noventa y dos

Ciento diez millones novecientos veintiseis mil novecientos veintisiete

Doscientos cincuenta y nueve millones cuatrocientos noventa y cinco mil sesenta y tres

Trescientos sesenta y dos millones ciento treinta y cinco mil quinientos cuarenta y seis

41

Novecientos cincuenta y cuatro millones ciento treinta y nueve mil doscientos cincuenta y nueve	Trescientos cincuenta y nueve millones doscientos noventa y un mil trescientos catorce

Cuatrocientos millones ochocientos setenta y un mil cuatrocientos veintitrés

Setecientos veintiún millones setecientos cincuenta y cinco mil seiscientos sesenta y siete

Novecientos cuarenta y nueve mil ochocientos noventa y seis mil novecientos veinticuatro

Ciento cincuenta millones trescientos sesenta y cinco seiscientos noventa y cinco

Seisientos cincuenta y cinco millones doscientos noventa y siete mil quinientos cincuenta y ocho

Cuatrocientos noventa y dos millones cuatrocientos noventa y ocho mil cincuenta

Write the following digits into written Spanish using their Cardinal and Ordinal.

Number	Ordinal	Cardinal
1	Uno	Primero
10435	Diez mil cuatrocientos treinta y cinto	Diezmilésimo cuadragésimo trigésimo quinto
3		
2		
6		
4		
9		
7		
8		
13		
16		
17		
12		
10		
18		
14		
11		
139		
708		

Género del Adjetivo (ADJECTIVE GENDER):

Most adjectives also have grammatical gender. Their gender is determined by the noun and all adjectives are masculine by default.

If the noun used doesn't explicitly presents its gender but the adjective allows for it, the speaker or writer has to specify themselves the noun's gender using only the adjective. Masculine adjectives are used in case the speaker doesn't know their gender either.

Nuestro supervisor es bueno — Our supervisor is good (It's implied that the speaker is male or a person of unknown gender)
Nuestra supervisora es buena — Our supervisor is good (It's implied that the speaker is female)

Adjective with their last letters being -o, -ete or -ote become feminine by replacing their very last letter with an -a.

Bonito — Pretty (male)
Bonita — Pretty (female)
Regordete — Chubby (male)
Regordeta — Chubby (female)
Grandote — Huge (male)
Grandote — Huge (female)

If they're finished with a consonant, they're turned feminine by placing an -a at the end of the word

Glotón — Glutton (male)
Glotona — Glutton (female)

People with their place of origin ending on -és, -uz, -án, and -in can be turned into feminine adjectives by adding an -a at the end.

Escosés — Scottish (male)
Escosesa — Scottish (female)
Andaluz — Andalusian (male)
Andaluza — Andalusian (female)
Alemán — German (male)
Alemana — German (female)
Mallorquín — Majorcan (male)
Mallorquina — Majorcan (female)

There are also adjectives that don't have a grammatical gender. Adjectives ending on -a, -e, -i, l, -u, -s, and -z on their base form do not use gender and are considered invariable. Adjectives ending with the syllables -ble, -bre-, -ente, -az, -iz, -oz, and -or. are also considered invariable adjectives.

Él es pacifista — He's pacifist.
Ella es pacifista — She's pacifist.
Él es valiente — He's brave
Ella es valiente — She's brave
El carro carmesí — Crimson car
La botella carmesí — Crimson bottle
El avión ágil — Agile plane
La patineta ágil — Agile skateboard
Él es hindú — He's Hindu.
Ella es hindú — She's Hindu.
El gato amigable — Friendly cat (male)
La gata amigable — Friendly cat (female)
El esposo pobre — Poor husband
La familia pobre — Poor family
El delfín inteligente — Smart dolphin
La lechuza inteligente — Smart Owl
El jefe capaz — Capable boss (male)
La gerente capaz — Capable manager (female)

El niño feliz — Happy little boy
La niña feliz — Happy little girl
La liebre veloz — Fast hare
El tren veloz — Fast train
El capítulo anterior — Previous chapter
La escena anterior — Previous scene

Número de los adjetivos (ADJECTIVE NUMBER)

In order to keep consistency, adjectives also adapt between singular and plural with their noun. These rules apply to both adjectives and nouns.

Adjectives finished with a unstressed vowel are added an -s at their end if they're needed to be plural.

El hombre cobarde — Cowardly man
Los hombres cobardes — Cowardly men
La moneda valiosa — Valuable coin
Las monedas valiosas — Valuable coins
El oso perezoso — Lazy bear
Los osos peresozos — Lazy bears

On the other hand, adjectives finished with a stressed vowel or a consonant will become plural by adding -es at the end.

La casa ideal — Ideal home
Las casas ideales — Ideal homes
El documento principal — Main document
Los documentos principales — Main documents
La manzana carmesí — Crimson apple
Las manzanas carmesíes — Crimson apples

Cómo preguntar en español (HOW TO ASK IN SPANISH):

The best way to learn anything is to ask questions, so what better way to learn Spanish than knowing how to make questions on their language?

Making "Yes" and "No" is as easy as taking a regular sentence and surround it with question marks. Unlike English, we neither need to modify any sentence structure nor add auxiliary verbs. We need to keep in mind, however, that Spanish uses an additional symbol when making question, and that is "¿".

Configuring your keyboard to use a Spanish layout will let you write "¿" using the second key next to zero (depending on keyboard or region). If you think this is a hassle and don't want to go through that, you can also type 168 on your numeric pad while holding Alt.

Marta camina por la acera — Marta walks on the pathway
¿Marta camina por la acera? — Does Marta walk on the pathway?
Pedro sabe historia — Pedro knows History
¿Pedro sabe historia? — Does Pedro knows History?
La lasaña está fría — The lasagna is cold
¿La lasaña está fría? — Is the lasagna cold?

"¿" marks the very beginning of the question so any commentary left outside question marks is considered context and not part of the question.

Mis nietos pueden comer huevos en la mañana, ¿pero también pueden comerlos de noche? — My grandchildren can eat eggs in the morning. But can they also eat them at night?

¿Mis nietos pueden comer huevos en la mañana, pero tambien pueden comerlos de noche? — Can my grandchildren eat eggs in the morning, but also eat them at night?

If we want to ask something a bit more complex than a "Yes" or "No" questions, something that require us to know a place, person, or amount, we need to take a look at Interrogative Pronouns. We use these at the very beginning of the sentence.

Most of them don't have a gender, but some of them do. In those cases, the gender of the pronoun needs to match those ones of the noun. "Cuanto" is singular only when talking about non-countable nouns. Countable nouns use instead its plural form, "Cuantos".

¿Qué? — What?
¿Qué haces? — What are you doing?
¿Qué están buscando? — What are they looking for?
¿Qué necesitas? — What do you need?
¿Qué piensas? — What do you think?

¿Cómo? — How?
¿Cómo estuvo tu día? — How was your day?
¿Cómo se sienten? — How are they feeling?
¿Cómo llego a la avenida principal? — How do I get to the main street?
¿Cómo resuelvo este rompecabezas? — How do I solve this puzzle?

¿Donde? — Where?
¿Donde están las salchichas? — Where are the weiners?
¿Donde comeremos hoy? — Where are we eating today?
¿A donde iremos de vacaciones? — Where are we going for vacations?
¿Donde puedo comprar una hamburguesa buena? — Where can I buy a good burger?

¿Cuando? — When?

¿Cuando vamos al parque? — When are we going to the park?

¿Cuando te dan tus notas? — When are you getting your grades?

¿Cuando empieza la película? — When is the movie starting?

¿Cuando viene tu tío? — When is your uncle coming?

¿Cual? ¿Cuales? — Which?

¿Cual es la montaña más alta del mundo? — Which is the tallest peak in the world?

¿Cual camisa debería ponerme? — Which shirt should I be wearing?

¿Cuales son los mejores juegos de mesa? — Which are the best tabletop games?

¿Cuales mascotas son las mejores para personas alérgicas? — Which pets are the best for allergic people?

¿Quién? ¿Quienes? — Who?

¿Quién es él? — Who is he?

¿Quién te dijo eso? — Who told you that?

¿Quienes trajeron refrigerios? — Who brought refreshments?

¿Quienes participarán en el torneo? — Who will participate in the tournament?

¿Cuanto? ¿Cuanta? ¿Cuantos? ¿Cuantas? — How much, how many

¿Cuanto tiempo ha pasado desde tu última visita? — How much time has passed since your last visit?

¿Cuanto oro llevará esa pieza? — How much gold will that piece have?

¿Cuantos cubitos de azucar quieres en tu té? — How many sugar cubes do you want on your tea?

¿Cuantos pájaros hay en ese cable? — How many birds are on that wire?

¿Cuanta madera necesito para una cabaña? — How much wood do I need for a cabin?

¿Cuanta paciencia necesito para ser niñera? — How much patience do I need to become a babysitter?

¿Cuantas fichas necesito para ganar? — How many tokens do I need to win?

¿Cuantas medallas necesito para ser famoso? — How many medals do I need to become famous?

Expresiones exclamatorias (EXCLAMATORY EXPRESSIONS):

Sometime when don't want to ask how great is something, rather, we want everyone to know how great that something is! For this, we use exclamatory expressions. Most of the time, all we have to do is place the pronoun "qué" right at the start, followed by an adjective or a noun.

¡Qué barato! — How cheap!
¡Qué dedicado! — How dedicated!
¡Qué tramposo! — What a cheater!
¡Qué abeja! — What a bee!

Saying something is outstanding is nice but other times we also want to be specific with our declarations. We can combine a noun with an adjective in order to make a better targeted expression about the noun's qualities.

The order in which we include the noun and its adjective in the sentence will influence how are we going to write the sentence. If we go adjective first, we write ¡Qué [adjective] [noun]!. If we go for the noun first, then we go ¡Qué [noun] [preposition tan/más] [adjective]!

¡Qué bonitas flores! — What beautiful flowers!
¡Qué flores más bonitas! — What beautiful flowers!

¡Qué original diseño! — What an original design!
¡Qué diseño más original! — What an original design!

¡Qué interesante documento! — What an interesting document!
¡Qué documento más interesante! — What an interesting document!

¡Qué sabroso pastel! — What a delicious cake!
¡Qué pastel tan sabroso! — What a delicious cake!

Just like interrogatory sentences, exclamatory expressions use an upside down exclamation mark to signal the beginning of the exclamation. To type it without any keyboard configuration we input 173 while holding Alt and then let the key go.

"Qué" isn't the only pronoun we can use. We can use "cómo" to emphasize how much endeavor is put into an action. For this, we need to use ¡Cómo [conjugated verb] [complement]!. Complement isn't necessary but it gives a great deal of information so it is recommended to use it.

¡Cómo comimos! — How we ate!
¡Cómo bailamos ayer! — How we danced yesterday!
¡Cómo saltó ese hombre la pared! — How that man jumped the wall!
¡Cómo te atreviste a decirles "no"! — How you dared to tell them "no"!

"Cuanto" is also used as an exclamation. It's used as an expression of marvel or dread towards the quantity of an object. To use is, we write ¡Cuanto [noun] [complement]!. Again, complement can be omitted but it can make our statement a lot more clear. "Cuanto" is affected by gender so we must use the grammatical gender of the word given.

"Cuanto" is also affected by quantity, but since we are marveling over an absurd amount we always consider the noun as plural. If we are talking about a countable noun, "Cuanto" becomes its plural, "Cuantos" or "Cuantas". Non-countable nouns stay singular.

¡Cuanto dinero! — So much money!

¡Cuanta carne! — So much meat!

¡Cuanto oro! — So much gold!

¡Cuanta comida! — So much food!

¡Cuanto moho! — So much mold!

¡Cuanta audiencia! — Ho much audience!

¡Cuantos perros! — So many dogs!

¡Cuantas aves! — So many birds!

¡Cuantos cangrejos! — So many crabs!

¡Cuantas personas! — So many people!

¡Cuantos huevos! — So many eggs!

¡Cuantas gallinas! — So many chickens!

Determinantes (DETERMINERS):

Determiners are words that give us additional information about the noun. They can be articles, possessive, demonstrative, numeral, indefinite, interrogative, or exclamatory. They are affected by gender and number

Articles are words used to determine whether or not we know something or someone. They can be either determined or undetermined. Determined demonstrative articles let us know we refer to a specific thing we know, when using undetermined articles we are talking about an object but it can be any object with the same name.

Articles	Determined		Undetermined	
Gender	Masculine	Feminine	Masculine	Feminine
Singular	El	La	Un	Una
Plural	Los	Las	Unos	Unas

La vecina trajo la sartén — The neighbor brought the frying pan
[It is implied we know which neighbor was supposed to bring us a frying pan we know about, maybe to borrow it to us or to have it returned.]

La vecina trajo una sartén — The neighbor brought a frying pan
[Here, a neighbor we expected brought with her a frying pan we know nothing about, probably as a gift or a product demostration]

Una vecina trajo la sartén — A neighbor brought the frying pan
[In this case, an unspecified neighbor of our brought a frying pan we were looking for, most likely as a lost item]

Una vecina trajo una sartén — A neighbor brought a frying pan
[A random neighbor of ours left us a frying pan. Maybe as a charity? Only she knows why in the world she would do that]

El niño trajo un perro — The boy brought a dog
Un niño trajo un perro — A boy brought a dog
Los niños trajeron un perro — The boys brought a dog
Unos niños trajeron un perro — Some boys brought a dog

Demonstrative articles let us know we are talking about a person, noun or object, that is at a certain distance. They express a vague distance of that object.

In English we have "This", "These", "That", and "Those". The first two are used to talk about an object at close distance, normally within reach; while the other two cover farther objects. In Spanish, however, we have three categories: Near (este), middle (ese), and far (aquello), each with their own pair of genders and numbers.

Demostratives	Near		Middle range		Far	
Gender	Masculine	Feminine	Masculine	Feminine	Masculine	Feminine
Singular	Este	Esta	Ese	Esa	Aquel	Aquella
Plural	Estos	Estas	Esos	Esas	Aquellos	Aquellas

"Este" is used just like its English counterpart, its use is given for objects within reach. "Ese" is used on objects that are out of reach but not far away (usually around 5m or around 16'50"). "Aquel" marks objects as further away than "ese", the minimum being around street-crossing distance. It can also be interpreted as "over there".

Esta pelota es mía — This ball is mine

[The speaker can place their hand on the ball]

Esa pelota es mía — That ball is mine
[The speaker can easily point their finger at the ball]

Aquella pelota es mía — That ball over there is mine
[The speaker can barely point at the direction their ball is supposed to be]

Este lápiz es de buena calidad — This pencil is of good quality
Esta jarra está llena de limonada — This jar is full of lemonade
Estos botones son de teclados viejos — These bottoms are from old keyboards
Estas galletas son para el picnic — These cookies are for the picnic

Ese árbol es muy alto — That tree is very tall
Esa mujer es muy bonita — That woman is very pretty
Esos patos devoran todo lo que ven — Those ducks devour everything they see
Esas ardillas están planeando algo — Those squirrels are up to something

Aquel hombre está haciendo guardia — That man over there is on guard duty
Aquella fuente es un pozo de lo deseos — That fountain over there is a wishing well
Aquellos hombres protestan con pancartas — Those men over there protest with signs
Aquellas palomas te asaltan si tienes pan — Those pigeons over there assault you if you have bread

Possessives point out something belongs or is related to someone. They determine if the noun is owned by multiple people and by whom.

Possessives	Single Owner				Multiple Owners			
Nº. nouns	Sigular		Plural		Singular		Plural	
Gender	Masculine	Feminine	Masculine	Feminine	Masculine	Feminine	Masculine	Feminine
1st person	Mío/Mi	Mía/Mi	Míos/Mis	Mías/Mis	Nuestro*	Nuestra*	Nuestros*	Nuestras*
2nd person	Tuyo/Tu	Tuya/Tu	Tuyos/Tus	Tuyas/Tus	Vuestro*	Vuestra*	Vuestros*	Vuestras*
3rd person	Suyo/Su	Suya/Su	Suyos/Sus	Suyas/Sus	Suyo/Su*	Suya/Su*	Suyos/Su*	Suya/Su*

*: Rules regarding plural persons may vary depending on the country. For more information, check "Pronombres Personales (PERSONAL PRONOUS)".

When used before after noun in possession, the determiner is used on its apocoped form, its shorter version. When used after the possessed noun, it is used on its full, longer form.

Este es mi tenedor — This is my fork
Este tenedor es mío — This fork is mine

Esta es mi casa — This is my house
Esta casa es mía — This house is mine

Ese es tu asiento — That is your sit
Ese asiento es tuyo — That sit is yours

Esta es tu manzana — This is your apple
Esta manzana es tuya — This apple is yours

Esos son mis cachorros — Those are my puppies
Esos cachorros son míos — Those puppies are mine

Esas son mis panquecas — Those are my pancakes
Esas panquecas son mías — Those pancakes are mine

Esos son tus cables — Those are your cables
Esos cables son tuyos — Those cables are yours

Esas son tus medias — Those are your socks
Esas medias son tuyas — Those socks are yours

Estas son sus servilletas — These are your napkins
Estas servilletas son suyas — These napkins are yours

Este es nuestro territorio — This is our territory
Este territorio es nuestro — This territory is ours

Esta es nuestra mascota — This is our pet
Esta mascota es nuestra — This pet is ours

Este es vuestro lugar — This is your place [informal plural]
Este lugar es vuestro — This place is yours [informal plural]

Esta es vuestra playa — This is your beach [informal plural]
Esta playa es vuestra — This beach is yours [informal plural]

Estos son nuestros refrigerios — These are our refreshers
Estos refrigerios son nuestros — These refreshers are ours

Estas son nuestras llaves — These are our keys
Estas llaves son nuestras — These keys are ours

Estos son vuestros regalos — These are your presents [informal plural]
Estos regalos son vuestros — These presents are yours [informal plural]

Estas son vuestras tareas — These are your tasks [informal plural]
Estas tareas son vuestras — These tasks are yours [informal plural]

The single formal version of you, "usted", and "ellos"; use the same conjugation as "el" and "ella". Context is necessary if we want to avoid confusion between them.

Este es su ticket, usted puede usarlo adentro — This is your ticket, you can use it inside.
Este ticket es suyo, usted puede usarlo adentro — This ticket is yours, you can use it inside

Yo entrego su paquete a Alejandro — I deliver his package to Alejandro
Yo entrego este paquete a Alejandro, es suyo — I deliver this package to Alejandro, it's his.

Ellos eligen su mascota — They choose their pet
Ellos eligen una mascota suya — They choose a pet of theirs

Possessive determiners can go right after the possessed noun. However, this form is mostly used on embellished Spanish pictured in poetry or literature, it's next to unused on colloquial Spanish.

Mi amigo — My friend
Amigo mío — Friend of mine
Mi esposa — My wife
Esposa mía — Wife of mine

Numerals determine the quantity, classification and order of a noun inside a sequence. They behave the exact same way numeral adjectives do so it is recommended you revisit numeral adjectives.

Seis manzanas — Six apples
Siete pecados — Seven sins
Ocho pedazos de pan — Eight pieces of bread
Nueve mangos — Nine mangos

Diez cerezas — Ten cherries

Sexto lugar — Sixth place
Séptimo cielo — Seventh heaven
Octava edición — Eighth edition
Novena nube — Nineth cloud

Interrogative determiners inform that the speakers is asking about something. They can be pronounced in a way they sound a interjection rather than a question. In that case, they become exclamatory determiners. Only "Cual" can't become an exclamatory determiner.

Interrogative	Sungular		Plural	
Gender	Masculine	Feminine	Masculine	Feminine
Which?	¿Cuál?	¿Cuál?	¿Cuáles?	¿Cuáles?
What?	¿Qué?	¿Qué?	¿Qué?	¿Qué?
What!	¡Qué!	¡Qué!	¡Qué!	¡Qué!
How much?	¿Cuánto?	¿Cuánta?	¿Cuántos?	¿Cuántas?
How much!	¡Cuánto!	¡Cuánta!	¡Cuántos!	¡Cuántas!

These are not to be confused with interrogative pronouns. Interrogative determiners are always next to a noun as a way to modify them into a unknown factor while interrogative pronouns are by themselves as an unknown noun we want answers for.

Determiner:
¿Cuanto dinero hay en el cochinito? — How much money is on the piggy bank?
Pronoun:

¿Cuanto hay en el cochinito? — How much is on the piggy bank?

Determiner:
¿Cuanto tiempo necesitas para acabar tu tarea? — How much time do you need to finish your homework?
¿Cuanto necesitas para acabar tu tarea? — How much do you need to finish your homework?

Determiner:
¿Qué oportunidad esperas para salir? — What oportunity are you waiting for to go out?
Pronoun:
¿Qué esperas para salir? — What are you waiting for to go out?

Determiner:
¿Qué botanas necesitas para tu reunión? — What snack do you need for your reunion?
Pronoun:
¿Qué necesitas para tu reunión? — What do you need for your reunion?

Pronombres personales (PERSONAL PRONOUNS):

Personal pronouns make reference to a person or an object without actually mention it on the sentence. They work very similar as personal pronouns in English but they have a few differences:

Since all non-abstracts nouns are considered either masculine or feminine, there no need for "it". it doesn't exist in Spanish.

There's multiple words for "you". While in English it's used to refer to any second person, Spanish uses multiple forms depending on which person we're referring to.

"Tú" is the informal singular version of "you", the formal version being "usted". In Spain, "vosotros" is used as an informal plural "you", and "ustedes" as an formal form. Most hispanic speakers however only use either "ustedes" or "vosotros" depending on their region, specially in latinamerica.

Yo — I
Tú — You (Singular, informal)
Usted — You (Singular, formal)
Ustedes — You (Plural, formal)
Él — He
Ella — She
Nosotros, nosotras — We
Vosotros, vosotras — You (plural, informal)
Ellos, ellas — They

EXERSICES:

Complete the following sentences with an interrogative determiner. Identify the tone of the speaker, the speaker may be using a exclamatory determiners instead.

Get a pen and a piece of paper and pay attention to the following sentences

Examples:
¿Cuanta mayonesa necesitas? — How much mayonnaise do you need?

¿Qué actividades piensas hacer? — What activities are you planning to do?

¡Cuanto dinero hay en esa cuenta! — How much money is on that account!

¿Cuales estudiantes son esos? — Which students are those?

¿Cuanta azucar tiene tu café? — How much sugar does your coffee have?

Now it's your turn:

¿_____ paletas son mía? — How many lollipops are mine?

¿_____ misión te llama la atención? — Which mission got your attention?

¡_____ hombre más molesto! — What an annoying man!

¿_____ español sabes? — How much Spanish do you know?

¡_____ sabe! — Who knows!

¿_____ quieres para cenar? — What do you want for dinner?

¿_____ cosas son las mejores en la vida? — What things are best in life?

¿_____ dinero te hace falta — How much money do you need?

¿_____ países hay en el mundo? — How many countries are in the world?

¿_____ personas necesitas para empezar una fiesta? — How many people do you need to start a party?

¿_____ animal es el más grande del mundo? — Which animal is the largest in the world?

¿Sabes _____ vamos a cocinar? — Do you know what are we going to cook?

¿_____ opinión tienes sobre el cambio climático? — What opinion do you have about climate change?

¿_____ sandwich debería llevar al picnic? — Which sandwich should I bring to the picnic?

¡_____ persona tan trabajadora! — What a hardworking person!

¿_____ agua tenemos? — How much water do we have?

¿_____ formato debería usar? — Which format do I use?

¿_____ vacas te pertenecen? — How many cows do you own?

¿_____ toppings para pizza aún no has comido? — Which pizza toppings haven't you eaten yet?

¿_____ navegador de internet me recomiendas? — Which internet browser do you recommend me?

¿_____ comida cabe en tu nevera? — How much food fits on your fridge?

¿_____ canción es tu favorita? — Which song is your favourite?

¿_____ verde es demasiado verded? — How much green is too much green?

¿_____ color de bigote le va mejor a la estátua? — Which moustache color looks better on the statue

¿_____ piso debemos considerar lava? — How much floor should we consider lava?

¿_____ velocidad tiene tu internet? — At what speed does your internet goes?

¿Por _____ tiempo prendes es aire acondicionado? — For how long do you turn on you air conditioner?

¿_____ temperatura tiene el sol? — What temperature does the sun have?

¿_____perro es un buen chico? — Which dog is a good boy?

¿_____ dinosaurio es tu favorito? — What dinosaur is your favourite?

¿_____chocolate cabe en tu boca? — How much chocolate fits in your mouth?

¿_____ tiempo de tu día usas para jugar? — How much time of your day you use to play?

¿_____ tipo de música te gusta? — What kind of music do you like?

¡_____ perro tan lindo! — What a cute dog!

¿_____ conocimiento tienes de economía? — How much knowledge do you have about economics?

¡_____ razón tienes! — How right you are!

¿_____ alumno quiere venir conmigo? — What student wants to come with me?

¿_____ locura crees que haces? — What madness do you think are you doing?

¿_____ huevos hay en un omelet? — How many eggs are in an omelette?

¡_____ caramelo más delicioso! — What a delicious candy!

¿_____ consejo es el peor que te han dado? — Which advice is the worst you had been given?

¿_____ cartas tenemos que hacer? — How many letters do we have to do?

¿_____ animadoras están listas? — How many cheerleaders are ready?

¿_____ problema tienes con nosotros? — What problem do you have with us?

¿_____ nota es la mejor de la clase? — What grades are the best of the class?

¿_____ tiempo debemos esperar? — How much time do we have to wait?

¿_____ lobos hacen una manada? — How many wolves make a pack?

Write the following groups of nouns and and adjectives in the correct order with their appropriate gender, number and demonstrative pronoun .

Adjective, noun (English)	Adjective, noun (Spanish)	Properly written noun with adjective
Fat, squirrel	Gordo, ardilla	La ardilla gorda
Loyal, dogs	Leal, perros	Los perros leales
First, place	Primero, lugar	El primer lugar
Sixth, chapter	Sexto, capítulo	El capítulo sexto
Heavy, bowl	Pesado, tazón	El tazón pesado, el pesado tazón
Second, opinion	Segundo, opinión	
Delicious, nuts	Delicioso, nueces	
Agile, eagle	Ágil, águila	
Furry, mice	Peludo, ratón	
Big, rat	Grande, rata	

Colombian, food	Colombiano, comida	
Shiny, stones	Brillante, piedras	
Murky, pathway	Lodoso, camino	
Hungry, opposum	Hambriento, zarigüeya	
Sly, fox	Ingenioso, zorro	
Tall, giraffe	Alto, jirafa	
Blue, pencil	Azul, pincel	
Dirty, eraser	Sucio, borrador	
Brazilian, dancer	Brasilero, bailarina	
Thick, books	Grueso, libros	
Hidden, trap	Oculto, trampa	
Narcissist, man	Narcisista, hombre	
Diligent, men	Diligente, hombres	
Fluffy, owls	Mullido, búhos	
Cold, water	Frío, agua	

Give the following words either a determined or undetermined if the word is (d) or (und) respectively.

Unos dados (und)	Un guante (und)	La profesora (d)	Los diamantes (d)
____ billetes (und)	____ promesa (und)	____ botones (und)	____ comunicación (d)
____ árbol (und)	____ personal (d)	____ abogado (d)	____ comunicado (und)
____ presidente (d)	____ terrenos (d)	____ sacerdote (und)	____ borregos (und)
____ cabello (und)	____ pantuflas (d)	____ estatua (und)	____ marea (d)
____ borrador (d)	____ comillas (d)	____ hoja (d)	____ preferencia (und)
____ teclados (d)	____ caracoles (und)	____ cometa (d)	____ semillas (und)
____ comida (d)	____ partículas (d)	____ caballero (und)	____ ratones (und)
____ lápiz (d)	____ basura (d)	____ espacio (d)	____ comercio (d)
____ pasillo (und)	____ costra (und)	____ pasto (d)	____ polilla (und)
____ paquetes (und)	____ cucaracha (und)	____ casas (und)	____ cigarros (und)
____ computadora (d)	____ pantera (und)	____ camisas (und)	____ helados (und)
____ papeles (und)	____ cebolla (d)	____ micrófono (d)	____ tomate (und)
____ costillas (d)	____ plátanos (und)	____ escoba (und)	____ colmena (und)
____ pincel (und)	____ espejo (d)	____ cojines (und)	____ csatillo (d)
____ porcelana (d)	____ plumas (und)	____ camello (und)	____ gatos (und)
____ loros (d)	____ letras (und)	____ hielo (d)	____ pintura (und)
____ zapato (d)	____ ciencia (d)	____ botas (d)	____ material (und)
____ comisiones (d)	____ cemento (d)	____ rango (d)	____ plegaria (und)
____ fogata (und)	____ pavimento (d)	____ pasarela (und)	____ costumbre (d)
____ marcador (und)	____ pastilla (und)	____ cepillo (und)	____ sierra (und)
____ medias (und)	____ cadena (und)	____ fecha (d)	____ papelera (und)

70

Give the following nouns their respective demonstrative determiners, taking into account the gender of the noun, their number, and if they're near (N), middle range (M), or far range (F) distance.

Estos____ (N) gatos son lindos — These cats are cute

Esos____ (M) gusanos son calvos — Those worms are bald

Aquellos (F) perros son mullidos — Those dogs are fluffy

_____ (N) alfombra es cara — This rug is expensive

_____ (N) son mis herramientas — These are my tools

A mí me gusta _____ (F) tipo de automóvil — I like that kind of automobile

_____ (N) animal es un erizo — This is a hedgehog

_____ (M) mujer es muy religiosa — That woman is very religious

Yo quiero _____ (N) niños lejos de mis galletas — I want those kids away from my cookies

_____ (F) día fue el peor — That day was the worst

_____ (M) leones dan miedo — Those lions are scary

Vanesa es bien conocida en _____ (N) lugar — Vanesa is well-known in this place

_____ (M) frutas son difíciles de cuidar — Those fruits are hard to take care of

71

La seguridad de _____ (M) carcel es muy alta — Security on that jail is very high

_____ (F) aquel niño es mi sobrino — That kid is my nephew

_____ (F) noches hacía mucho frío — Those nights were cold

_____ (M) trabajadores son profesionales — Those workers are professionals

Mi mamá adora _____ (M) marca de café — My mom loves that brand of coffee

_____ (F) vez fue un error — That time was a mistake

_____ (M) hombre es un desconocido — That man is a stranger

_____ (M) es la política de _____ (N) lugar — Those are the politics of this place

_____ (M) ratas parecen zarigüeyas — Those rats look like racoons

_____ (M) empresa estafa seguido — That company scams often

Pronombres de Objeto Directo (DIRECT OBJECT PRONOUNS):

Just like personal pronouns, they take the role of replacing an object with a pronoun. However, instead of replacing the noun they change the direct object of the sentence, the part that receives the action made by a noun using a transitive verb.

Assuming we know who is doing what to who, we can make a sentence only using personal pronoun, verb, and direct object pronoun.

Lola adora el helado — Lola adores ice cream
Ella adora el helado — She adores ice cream
Lola lo adora — Lola adores it
Ella lo adora — She adores it

Pedro quiere la galleta — Pedro wants the cookie
Él quiere la galleta — He wants the cookie
Pedro la quiere — Pedro wants it
Él la quiere — He wants it

Luis tiene muchos regalos — Luis has lots of gifts
Él tiene muchos regalos — He has lots of gifts
Luis los tiene — Luis has them
Él los tiene — He has them

Maria viste a sus muñecas — Maria dresses her dolls
Ella viste a sus muñecas — She dresses her dolls
Maria las viste — María dresses them
Ella las viste — She dresses them

There's also indirect object pronouns. When using indirect object, the noun is performing an action on an object, which is used to interact with another object. This other object is the indirect object.

Pablo leyó un libro a Daniel — Pablo read a book to Daniel
Pablo le leyó un libro — Pablo read a book to him

Gabriel prestó una pelota a Luci — Gabriel lend a ball to Lucy
Gabriel le prestó una pelota — Gabriel lend her a ball

A word of caution: There must be a previous understanding of what nouns we are talking about before using pronoun, nouns, or object nouns. If we say "he got it" before ever talking about Sergio getting his meal, we'll just confuse our listener.

EXCERSICES:

Replace the direct object or the indirect object of the following sentences.
Mateo tiene la pelota — Mateo la tiene

Luis confía en Érica — Luis confía en ella

Las gemelas saben matemáticas — Las gemelas las saben

Julio conoce a todos los clientes de su papá —Julio le conoce a todos sus clientes

Lila ayudó con su tarea a su hermana — Lila la ayudó con su tarea

Tu hija necesita tu atención — _____

A Roberto no le gustan los perros — _____

Lila detesta la harina de trigo — _____

Los audífonos de esa marca son buenos — _____

El control lo tiene Ronald — _____

Benito tiene una carta de colección — _____

El perro cava en el jardín — _____

El vecino tiene flores hermosas — _____

El empleado no tiene la culpa — _____

Mi papá toma cerveza — _____

Jorge limpia el horno — _____

Mi papá odia la burocracia — _____

Gustavo empuja piedras fuera del camino —

_____

Núñez corta árboles muy grandes —

_____

Ellos odian las nueces — _____

Fátima sabe tocar la gaita — _____

La ensalada incluye tomate, lechuga y huevos —

_____

Francisco juega ajedrez con Daniela — _____

Simón cabalga en un caballo blanco — _____

Pablo compra un televisor por internet — _____

Anastasia tiene alergia — _____

Carla fue a la playa con Manuela — _____

Las vacas adoran el pasto — _____

Valeria cabalga el poni de Pietro — _____

Julián está cansado de compartir cuarto con Anabel —

_____

Cristóbal le dio su tarea al profesor — _____

Miguel saltó la cerca antes que Juan — _____

El pie de Estevan tiene un callo enorme —

_____

Ben invitó a Isabel a pasear — _____

Ortega tiene el compás de Juana — _____

Mis instrucciones son mejores que las de Alberto —

_____

Lisandro le da caramelos a sus hermanos menores —

_____

La iglesia de la comunidad adora a San Antonio —

_____

Colombia tiene mucha gente simpática —

_____

La primavera trajo flores, abejas y miel —

_____

Victoria trajo queso de prueba para Marcos —

_____

Estás sandalias se llenaron de arena —

_____

La vida está llena de cosas buenas y malas —

_____

Yo presté mis guantes a Carolina — _____

Negación (NEGATION):

Making a positive tense into a negative one is something that is slightly easier to do in Spanish than in English. The majority of the time, all you have to do is to place "no" right before the verb.

Pedro ve películas románticas — Pedro watches romantic movies
Pedro no ve películas de horror — Pedro doesn't watch horror movies

Paula juega voleibol — Paula plays volleyball
Paula no juega damas chinas — Paula doesn't play checkers

Yo como mucha carne — I eat a lot of meat
Yo no como muchos vegetales — I don't eat a lot of vegetables

Mis estudiantes van juntos a la playa — My students go together to the beach
Mis estudiantes no van juntos al cine — My students don't go together to the movies

Nosotros reunimos dinero para comprar instrumentos — We save money to buy instruments
Nosotros no reunimos dinero para comprar helado — We don't save money to buy ice cream

When we are making a sentence that has a direct or indirect object pronoun right behind the verb, we cannot separate them, which is usually the case for sentences that have the noun doing the action of the verb to itself. For these cases, we place "no" behind the pronoun instead.

Pietro me llamó para reunirnos — Pietro called me to hang out
Melisa no me llamó para reunirnos — Melisa didn't call me to hang out

Mamá me regañó por gastar de más — Mom scolded me for buying too much
Mamá no me regañó por traer bananas — Mom didn't scold me for bringing bananas

Tú me haces un favor — You make me a favor
Tú no me haces enojar — You don't make me angry

Clarisa me dio un beso — Clarisa gave me a kiss
Elena no me dio un beso — Elene didn't give me a kiss

There's also a handful of words we can use to express something on a negative sense without using "no". These words and their positive counterparts are:

Algo — Something
Nada — Nothing

Algo falta en esta pintura — Something is missing on this painting
Nada falta en esta pintura — Nothing is missing on this painting
Algo extraño pasa en el vecindario — Something strange is happening in the neighborhood
Nada extraño pasa en el vecindario — Nothing strange is happening in the neighborhood

Alguien — Someone
Nadie — Nobody

Alguien vino a verme esta tarde — Someone came to see me this afternoon
Nadie vino a verme esta tarde — Nobody came to see me this afternoon
Alguien nos ayuda con nuestras entrega — Someone is helping us with our deliveries

Nadie nos ayuda con nuestras entregas — Nobody is helping us with our deliveries

Siempre — Always
Nunca — Never
Jamás — Never, ever

Siempre me lavo las manos antes de escribir — I always wash my hands before writing
Nunca me lavo las manos antes de escribir — I never wash my hands before writing
Siempre te quedas con la mejor parte — You always get the best part
Nunca te quedas con la mejor parte — You never get the best part

También — Also, too
Tampoco — Neither

Diana juega golf, ella también juega tenis — Diana plays golf, she also plays tennis
Diana no juega golf, ella tampoco juega tenis — Diana doesn't play golf, neither she plays tennis
Juan sabe tocar el piano, él también toca la guitarra — Juan knows how to play the piano, he plays the guitar too
Juan no sabe tocar el piano, él tampoco toca la guitarra — Juan doesn't know how to play the piano, neither he plays the guitar

O ... o — Either .... or
Ni ... ni — Neither ... nor

O te quedas o nos vamos — Either you stay or we leave
Ni te quedas ni nos vamos — Neither you stay nor we leave
O lavas tu ropa o me prestas la lavadora — Either you wash your clothes or you let me borrow the washing machine
Ni lavas tu ropa ni me prestas la lavadora — Neither you wash your clothes nor you let me borrow the washing machine

Algún, alguno, alguna, algunos, algunas — Some, something
Ningún, ninguno, ninguna, ningunos, ningunas — None, no

Algunos de mis perros tienen garrapatas — Some of my dogs has ticks
Ninguno de mis perros tiene garrapatas — None of my dogs have ticks
Algunas maletas vienen con ruedas — Some suitcases come with wheels
Ninguna maleta viene con ruedas — No suitcase comes with wheels

We can use those negative words as a more expressive version of "no" and place them right behind the verb, or use the as a negative pronoun.

Manuela no vino a mi casa — Manuela didn't come to my house
Nadie vino a mi casa — Nobody came to my house

Unlike English, Spanish doesn't have the concept of double negatives. You can use as many negative words as you want in the same sentence and it still will be negative.

Alicia dio su número de teléfono — Alicia gave her phone number
Alicia no dio su número de teléfono — Alicia didn't give her phone number
Alicia no dio su número de teléfono a nadie — Alicia didn't give her phone number to anyone
Alicia no dio nunca su número de teléfono a nadie — Alicia never gave her phone number to anyone.

As silly as they may look, they're all correct negative sentences. In translation we can only bring a single negative to English or use them on separate sentences to keep consistency with the negativity. This usually only emphasizes how much an action did not happen.

Negatives words have no gender except for "ninguno". They're the only ones that need to keep consistency with their respective noun or object. When used right next to a masculine object, they drop their termination -o.

Ramón no recuerda ningún cuento — Ramón doesn't remember any tale
Él tampoco recuerda ninguna fábula — He doesn't remember any fable either

Julio no tiene ningún libro en su tienda — Julio doesn't have any books on his store
Él tampoco tiene ninguna película — He doesn't have any movies either

Since "ninguno" expresses a lack of something, they're only expressed in singular. They're only plural if the noun can only exist as a plural, even then it still sounds awkward to native speakers so it's not widely used. Alternate uses that doesn't use "ningunos" or ningunas" are preferred on those cases.

Ningunas fáuces romperán estos guanteletes — No jaws can break these gauntlets
No hay fauces que rompan estos guanteletes — There's no jaws that can break these gauntlets

Pronombres y preposiciones
(PRONOUNS AND PREPOSITIONS):

Prepositions are words used to link two or more words together with the purpose of giving them more sense. They can be used to clarify motives, parting points, directions, destinations, among other similar things.

Manuel salió a Colombia — Manuel went to Colombia
Manuel salió de Colombia — Manuel left Colombia
Manuel salió desde Colombia — Manuel left from Colombia

In this book we're going to list the most common use of prepositions. If you still don't have much exposure with Spanish, it is recommended you give a closer look to them, as they can vastly change the meaning of a sentence if not used properly.

"de": It can mean either "of", "from", or "about". This preposition has a lot of uses and is in fact one of the most, if not the most used in Spanish. It's used to determine ownership, nationality, topics, causes, the material of an object, and time of day.

Ese es el muñeco de Felipe — That's Felipe's toy
Soy de Chile — I'm from Chile
Mi papá no sabe nada de computadoras — My dad knows nothing about computers
Diana se aburrió de ver las Luchas — Diana got bored of watching the Luchas
Mi abuelo tiene un trofeo de oro — My grandfather has a gold medal
Nosotros no dormimos de día — We don't sleep at night
Son las tres de la tarde — It's three o'clock

Sometimes "de" will be behind "el" prepositions. Since both have their "e" in common right next to each other, both words merge into a single word, "del". The merging of those two words is mandatory.

El empleado de el banco (Wrong)
El empleado del banco

"a": It's mostly compared to "to" and "at", but it has many more applications. It's used when the direct object refers to a person or a humanized direct object like pets or sentient beings. It's also used to express directs objects regarding scale, location, and directions; or giving a specific time.

María saluda a Teresa — María greets Teresa
Hay un semáforo a diez metros — There's a traffic light at ten meters
Carlos fue a la derecha — Carlos went to the right
Estevan se mudó a Panamá — Estevan moved to Panama
La reuinón es a las cuatro — The reunion is at four o'clock

Preposition "a" also merges together with "el", making the word "al". Just like "del", it is incorrect to say or write "a el".

De la ciudad a el campo (Wrong)
De la ciudad al campo

"en": Can be roughly translated as "in", "on", and "at". Spanish doesn't make a distinction between "in", "on", and "at" so "en" works the same for either of them. We use it to indicate locations, and broad times like months, years, and seasons. More specific times of the day like hours or days of the week use "a" instead.

...en Londres — at London
...en la puerta — at the door
...en primavera — in spring
...en 1987 — in 1987
...en la sala — in the living room
...en enero — in January

We also use "en" we talking about methods of transport like plane, bus, or car. However, there are two exceptions to this rule: When we travel by foot or by horse, we use "a" instead.

Nosotros viajamos... — We traveled
...en avión — by plane
...en barco — by boat
...a pie — by foot
...a caballo — by horse

"por": Another preposition of many uses. Fortunately, It can be mostly translated as "because of", "by", and "for" in most cases. It is used when indicating a cause, a reason, a exchange, showing support for a person, multiplication, or as a direct translation of the word "per".

Yo me mojé por el clima — I got wet because of the weather
Mina pasea por la noche — Mina strolls by nighttime
Ronda lo hizo por amor — Ronda did it for love
Lila compró una malteada por cinco dólares — Lila bought a milkshake for five dollars
Sergio votó por su candidato — Sergio voted for his candidate
Cinco por dos son diez — Five times two equals ten
Un vaso por persona — A cup per person

"con": This preposition is a very direct translation to "with". It is used when the noun doesn't do the action of the verb on its own. It expresses company and the use of either the direct or indirect object as a tool. "con" always goes right behind the companion.

Enrique fue al cine con Helena — Enrique went to the movies with Helena
Luis dibuja con un pincel — Luis draws with a brush
Marisa come arroz con palillos — Marisa eats rice with chopsticks

"sin": This is a direct translation for the word "without", much like it's positive counterpart "with". It is only used when expressing a lack of something or someone.

Pablo hizo la tarea sin ayuda — Pablo did his homework without help
Lucia está triste sin tu presencia — Lucia is sad without your presence

"para": It translates as "for", or "to". "para" is used to indicate a target, may it be a goal or a person. Specifically, it's used for setting a purpose, destination, addressee, and deadlines.

El trapo es para limpiar la mesa — The cloth is for cleaning the table
El trabajo es para mañana — The assignment if for tomorrow
Pepe va para el parque — Pepe goes to the park
Este regalo es para mamá — This gift is for mom

"sobre": It's translated mostly as "above", "about", or synonyms of those two words. It's two purposes are to indicate the noun is above an object and to set the object as a topic.

El gato duerme sobre la silla — The cat sleeps on the table
El caballo saltó sobre la cerca — The horse jumped over the fence
Lisa sabe mucho sobre historia — Lisa knows a lot about History

Occasionally, this word also functions as a noun that means envelope, as inpacket, wrapper, or post. Almost all the time it is used as a preposition, but there's also a possibility of it showing up as a noun.

El sobre tiene una revista sobre aves — The envelope has a magazine about birds

"hasta": It translate mainly as "up to" and "until". It's used to indicate a limit to the verb.

Fernando trabaja hasta la noche — Fernando works until night
Jonás puede comer hasta ocho kilos de jamón — Jonás can eat up to eight kilograms of ham
El bus está detenido hasta las cuatro — The bus is stopped until four [o'clock]

"entre": Can be read as "between" and "among". It's used to let us know something has been included on a group of other things. Depending on the context, it may be in the middle of them.

Nosotros pagamos el hospedaje entre todos — We paid the lodging between everybody
Las geodas se esconden entre las piedras — Geodes hide among the rocks
Las cucharas están entre los tenedores y los cuchillos — The spoons are between the forks and knives

"desde": It's used as "from" or "since". It indicates the action is taking place from a starting point either in time or space.

La abuela ha vivido aquí desde los cincuentas — Grandmother has lived here since the fifties
Los turistas entran desde Colombia — Tourists come in from Colombia

"hacia": It can be translated literally as "towards". We use it when we tell something is facing a direction with a generalized point of reference. It can also be use when expressing emotions directer to a person.

Luis miró hacia su derecha — Luis looked toward his right
Yo caminé hacia el parque — I walked towards the park
Pablo siente respeto hacia su profesor — Pablo feels respect towards his teacher

"contra": Translates literally as "against". It's used to express opposition, it can physical against an object, against abstract objects, or it could be an strife between two or more individuals or factions.

Valeria está contra el muro — Valeria is against the wall
Miguel está contra el aborto — Miguel is against abortion
Mi grupo contra tu grupo — My group against your group

"bajo": It hard translates as "under". It's used when the object is below or influenced by another object. Those objects can both be concrete or abstract.

El gato duerme bajo la mesa — The cat sleeps under the table
Mi sobrina está bajo mi cuidado — My niece is under my care
La asociación está bajo investigación — The association is under investigation

"ante": It translates as "before", but only in a sense of presence. It means something is right in front of something else.

Carmen se presenta ante la junta — Carmen appears before the board
Gilberto pelea ante su maestro — Gilberto fights before his teacher
La villa se prepara ante una hambruna — The village prepares before a famine

"según": It's translates literally as "according to". It's used when expressing an opinion coming from a third party.

El tomate es muy saludable según los expertos — Tomatoes are very healthy according to experts
Según tú, yo tengo depresión — According to you, I have depression

"tras": This preposition translates a s "after" or "behind", as strange as it may sound. "tras" means "after" when we talk about time or chases, but it means "behind" when talking about space.

El frío quedó tras irse el invierno — The cold stayed after winter left
La policía fue tras el ladrón — The police went after the thief
Linda está escondida tras la cortina — Linda is hidden behind the curtain.

"mediante": It translates a "through", and it's used to present formally a methodology or means of control.

El grupo de Guillermo está mejor organizado mediante las nuevas reglas — Guillermo's group is better organized through the new rules
El tanque controla la presión mediante valvulas automáticas — The tank controls its pressure through automated valves

"durante": Translates literally as "during". It's used to point out simultaneity or parallelism of an event with another

Carla tomó mucho durante la fiesta — Carla drank too much during the party

"versus": It's the same as in English, it's only use is to set two parts in a conflicting mode. It can be used as a synonym for "contra" when talking about objects in a match.

La pelea de hoy será Perez versus Jiménez — Today's fight will be Perez versus Jiménez

"vía": This preposition translates as "through". Much like "mediante", both of them are used to present a methodology in which something is done, it is mostly used when traveling or sending parcels, though. Vía's main use is to let us know something is done by passing through something first.

Luis mandó el paquete via avión — Luis sent the package through plain
Los Gonzales llegaron a Caracas via Valencia — The Gonzales made it to Caracas through Valencia

In some cases, preposition "de" gets together with another word and forms what is known as compound prepositions. Their only use is to tell the location of an object relative to another. The merging rules for "del" still apply.

"delante de": It means "in front of" and it's made when merging "ante" and "de". It's used when we want to say the object is facing another.

Clara se sienta delante de Rodrigo — Clara sits in front of Rodrigo

"detrás de": It translates as "behind" and is made when combining "trás" and "de". It's the contrary of "delante de", it announces when something is on the opposite side of their front.

Hay un perro detrás de Diego — There's a dog behind Diego

"encima de": When combining "encima" and "de" we get a word that translates as "on", as in "above". We use this when an object is right over another, usually by laying there, stepping on it, or just making pressure over it. Its use is normally reserved when the object does not belong on that position.

Mi gato se sienta encima del tuyo — My cat sits on yours

"enfrente de": It translates as "in front of". It works much like "delante de", but we use it only if the object is on direct proximity to the other.

El caballo se paró enfrente de Daniel — The horse stopped in front of Daniel

There are some exceptions to the rule. There are three words that, when combined with "en", do not translated literally and work like idioms, those are "en vivo", "en serio", and "en broma".

"En vivo" translates as live, as in a direct transition.

Nuestro canal está en vivo desde Aruba — Our channel is live from Aruba

En serio" translates as, "seriously" or "being serious".

Pablo habla en serio sobre la anciana — Pablo is serious about the old lady
En serio, eso no es gracioso — Seriously, that's not funny

"En broma" translates as "kidding" or "as a joke".

Yo lo digo en broma — I'm kidding/I said it as a joke

Some prepositions can be used alongside pronouns too to give the sentence more concrete meaning. When doing this, "Yo" is replaced by "Mí" and "Tú" is replaced by "Tí". The structure for this composition is Preposition + Pronoun.

Ellos me hablaron de tí — They talked to me about you
Yo participé por él — I participated for him
Mi mamá se hartó de tí — My mom got tired of you
Nadie sabe nada de mí — Nobody knows anything about me

The prepositions usable with pronouns are "a" (to), "en" (in/on/at), "de" (of/from/about), "para" (for), and "entre" (between).

Papa fue a la casa a buscar algo — Dad went home looking for something
Patricia está en camino — Patricia is on her way
Mi hermana está en problemas — My sister is in trouble
Yo estoy en el trabajo — I am at work
Ese regalo es para tí — That gift is for you
Paula está entre Pepe y Pablo — Paula is between Pepe and Pablo

"Con" can be used as well but when used with "Mí" and "Tí" they combine into a single word. They become "Conmigo" and "Contigo" respectively. The rest of the pronouns stay the same and separated from their preposition.

Yo estoy enojado contigo — I am angry with you
Marlene quiere salir en una cita contigo — Marlene want to go out on a date with you
Todo se puede conmigo — Everything is possible with me
Conmigo las fiestas jamás son aburridas — With me parties are never boring

You might have noticed some of the prepositions have the same uses on some situations even if they're different. Some of them can be interchanged and not affect the meaning of the message. Others might keep the same message but will drift the reader or listener's attention to some other parts of the sentence. Try to make it so the message you want to deliver doesn't warp in the process when using prepositions.

En el torneo tenemos a Claudia versus Tina — At the tournament we have Claudia versus Tina
En el torneo tenemos a Claudia contra Tina — At the tournament we have Claudia against Tina

El pájaro está enfrente de tí — The bird is in front of you
El pájaro está delante de ti — The bird is [right] in front of you

Nosotros llegamos al norte via México — We made it north through Mexico
Nosotros llegamos al norte desde México — We made it north from México

EXERSICES:

Get a pen and a piece of paper and complete the following sentences using the correct preposition for the situation given.

Example: Matías espera en frente de la puerta — Matías waits in front of the door

Example: María está enamorada de Francisco — María is in love with Francisco

Yo tengo un regalo _____ Lucía — I have a gift for Lucía

Sergio está ahí _____ ayudarte — Sergio is there to help you

Papá dejó un sobre _____ la mesa — Dad left an envelope on the table

Todos los hombres son cerdos _____ mi mamá — All men are pigs according to my mom

Pedro caminó _____ su casa _____ la mía — Pedro walked from his house to mine

Mi perro juega al Frisbi _____ parar — Mi dog plays Frisbee nonstop

La toalla se secó _____ recibir tanto sol — The towel dried after getting so much sunlight

Tu loro duerme _____ periódico — Your parrot sleeps on top of the newspapers

Mi familia recibió un paquete _____ la abuela — My family recieved a package from grandma

Carlos te dará un juguete _____ su DVD — Carlos will give you a toy for his DVD

Jorge le dio un cachorro _____ Paula — Jorge gave a puppy to Paula

Tus anteojos son _____ calidad — Your glasses are of quality

Sabriná está _____ mi — Sabrina is behind me

Todos los ratones huyen _____ la gente — All mice run away from people

Yo fui _____ mis amigos _____ cine _____ bus — I went to the

94

movies with my friends on bus

Jaime fue _____ la iglesia — Jaime went to the Church

Mamá no sabe trabajar _____ presión — Mom doesn't know how to work under pressure

Liliana se unió a una organización _____ el SIDA — Liliana joined an organization againts HIV

El letrero se cayó _____ instalarlo — The sign fell after installing it

La gerente está de mal humor — The manager is on a bad mood

El viaje lo hacemos _____ la carretera — The travel is made through the highway

Pepe piensa comer _____ la fiesta — Pepe plans to eat during the party

Tú tienes un animal _____ la mesa — You have an animal under the table

Los cuchillos _____ tu casa son _____ plata — Your home's knives are made of silver

No tengo uso _____ tu investigación — I have no use for your investigation

Tus primos son _____ Argentina — Your cousins are from Argentina

Helga está cansada _____ correr — Helga is tired of running

Su tío trabaja _____ su bienestar — Their uncle works for their well-being

La jaula está llena _____ canarios — The cage is full of canaries

Pamela quiere un pastel _____ leche — Pamela wants a pastry with milk

Sandra quiere un pastel _____ leche — Sandra wants a milk cake

La tienda _____ Mario está abierta _____ las siete _____ la mañana — Mario's store is open since 7 o'clock

Mi hermanito está _____ en problemas — My little brother is in trouble

Nadie puede estar _____ mostrador — Nobody can be behind the counter

Tu cabeza está llena _____ tonterías — Your head is full of silliness

Rafael reporta el huracán en vivo — Rafael reports the hurricane live

Alberto responde sus preguntas _____ ingenio — Alberto answers his questions with ingenuity

Las fiestas _____ año nuevo son _____ diciembre y enero — New Year's parties are between December and January

La casa se siente sola _____ tí — The house feel lonely without you

El pavo está en la cocina — The turkey is in the kitchen

Los peces solo pueden vivir dentro _____ agua —Fish can only live under water

Las donas están llenas _____ jalea — The donuts are filled with jelly

Nátali no sabe dibujar _____ pintura — Nátali doesn't know how to draw with paint

Las galletas _____ arroz son mejores que las _____ trigo — Rice cookies are better than wheat ones.

Las calles están llenas _____ cangrejos — The streets are full of crabs

Mama cuenta _____ — Mom counts with you

El perro de Luis salta cuando está _____ — Luis' dog jumps when he's with me

Verbo (VERB):

This word explains an action, state, or events centered around the noun. Just like in English, Spanish possesses verbs that are regular and irregular when it comes to their conjugation. It is recommended that you learn irregular verbs so you know which ones you can use regular verb conjugation on.

Regular verbs are those which follow a common pattern when conjugated. In English, those verbs are those who add -s to the third person, -ed for past and past participle, and -ing for gerund. Irregular verbs don't follow these rules. The vast majority of verbs are regular, though those of most common use are irregular. Rules for verbs in Spanish are by far much more complex than that.

Conjugación (CONJUGATION):

In order for us to use a verb properly, we must change it in order to match the person we want to communicate to, the number of people mentioned and at what time the verb is making mention of.

The first is step is to identify person we are referring to. Fortunately, this works the same as in English.

Person	Singular	Plural
First Person	Yo (I)	Nosotros (We)*
Second Person	Tú (You)	Ustedes/Vosotros (You)*
Third Person	Él/Ella (He/Her)	Ellos/Ellas (They)*

*: Remember the rules regarding plural persons when used on some countries. For a refresher, reread "Pronombres Personales (PERSONAL PRONOUNS)".

Then we take the verb and modify as necessary taking into account its infinitive (base) form. While English identify their infinitive verbs using the preposition 'to' (to take, to sew, to make), Spanish uses a single word which ends on either -ar, -er, or -ir.

Lastly, we replace -ar, -er, or -ir with the termination needed for the verb to satisfy the use of a first, second, or third person on either singular or plural form.

There are a lot of ways to conjugate verbs. For the sake of simplicity and to give a proper example, we'll only use their most common, simple forms as an example.

Terminación '-ar'	Presente	Pretérito	Imperfecto	Futuro
Yo	-o	-é	-ába	-eré
Tú	-as	-áste	-ábas	-ás
Él, ella, usted	-a	-ó	-ába	-á
Nosotros/as	-ámos	-ámos	-ábamos	-émos
Vosotros/as	-áis	-teis	-ábais	-éis
Ellos/as, ustedes	-an	-ron	-ában	-án

Terminación '-er'	Presente	Pretérito	Imperfecto	Futuro
Yo	-o	-í	-ía	-eré
Tú	-es	-iste	-ías	-rás
Él, ella, usted	-e	-ió	-ía	-erá
Nosotros/as	-emos	-ímos	-íamos	-eremos
Vosotros/as	-éis	-isteis	-íais	-eréis
Ellos/as, ustedes	-en	-ieron	-ían	-erán

Terminación '-ir'	Presente	Pretérito	Imperfecto	Futuro
Yo	-o	-í	-ía	-iré
Tú	-es	-iste	-ías	-irás
Él, ella, usted	-e	-ió	-ía	-irá
Nosotros/as	-ímos	-imos	-íamos	-íremos
Vosotros/as	-ís	-isteis	-íais	-iréis
Ellos/as, ustedes	-en	-ieron	-ían	-irán

Presente del indicativo (PRESENT INDICATIVE):

Present indicative is the most common and simple form of the verb. It has many uses, but its main purpose is to indicate the doing of an action.

It is used when we are talking about facts:

Elvira quiere comer — Elvira wants to eat
Sergio construye una presa — Sergio builds a dam
Cristian camina lento — Cristian walks slow
Crístofer está solo en casa — Cristofer is alone at home

It expresses routines:

Nosotros compartimos con nuestros vecinos todos los días — We share with our with our niehgbors everyday
Mi mamá prepara el desayuno en las mañanas — My mom prepares breakfast in the morning
Mis amigos y yo jugamos en mi casa los sábados — My friends and me play at my place on Saturdays
Ramón bebe café después de levantarse — Ramón drinks coffee after getting up

It explains for how long the action in question has been going:

Mi hijo ahorra dinero desde los 4 años — My son has been saving money since he was 4 years old
Yo riego mi patio desde hace una década — I've been watering my lawn since a decade ago
Soy un fanático del deporte desde pequeño — I've been a sport fan since I was little
Benito ayuda a sus amigos desde que ellos lo ayudaron — Benito has been helping his friend since they helped him

Conjugación para verbos regulares
(CONJUGATION FOR REGULAR VERBS):

Persona	Terminación -ar	Terminación -er	Terminación -ir
Yo	-o	-o	-o
Tú	-as	-es	-es
Él, ella, usted	-a	-e	-e
Nosotros/as	-amos	-emos	-imos
Vosotros/as	-áis	-éis	-ís
Ellos/as, ustedes	-an	-en	-en

Yo pinto la cerca de blanco — I paint the fence white
Tú pisas barro con tus zapatos nuevos — You step on mud with your new shoes
Él cambia un libro por otro — He changes a book for another
Notrotros prestamos ayuda veterinaria — We offer veterinary help
Vosotros cobráis muy caro — You charge too much.
Ellos atrapan insectos por diversión — They catch bugs for fun

Yo comprendo tu frustración — I understand your frustration
Tú toces cada vez que salimos — You cough whenever we go out
Ella recoge basura en su patio — She picks up trash on her backyard
Nosotros protegemos el vecindario — We protect the neighborhood
Vosotros hacéis buena pareja — You make a good couple
Ellos merecen otra oportunidad — They deserve another chance

Yo vivo junto a César — I live next to César
Tú compartes habitación con tu hermano — You share your room with your brother
Usted divide muy bien las rebanadas de pastel — You divide very

well the slices of cake

Nosotros reímos a todo pulmón — We laugh at the top of our lungs

Vosotros dormís profundamente — You sleep deeply

Ellos mugen cuando ven vacas — They moo when they see cows

Excepciones y verbos irregulares (EXCEPTIONS AND IRREGULAR VERBS):

While regular verbs are very straightforward on how they're handled, keep in mind Spanish has many exceptions to these rules. Make sure to check if the verb in question is regular or irregular.

There are irregular verb that only show their irregularity with their singular first person (Yo). The rest of their conjugation goes as normal.

Persona	Dar	Traer	Salir
Yo	Doy	Traigo	Salgo
Tú	Das	Traes	Sales
Él, ella usted	Da	Trae	Sale
Nosotros/as	Damos	Traemos	Salimos
Vosotros/as	Dáis	Traéis	Salís
Ellos/as, ustedes	Dan	Traen	Salen

Verbos con alteración vocálica (VERBS WITH VOCALIC ALTERATION):

We also run into verbs that are irregular on their conjugation because there are grammatical rules that change the way they are conjugated in comparison to other regular verbs. The placement of certain letters on the second to last syllable makes it so it's necessary to change the way how those sounds are pronounced.

Verbs ending on -ar, -er-, or -ir still have their regular verb rules of conjugation. However, changes are made to its root in all persons except "nosotros" and "vosotros" (We).

When the verb is a word which its second to last syllable has the vowel "e" on it but it's not the final letter of the root, we change that "e" for "ie".

Persona	Confesar	Atender	Sentir
Yo	Confieso	Atiendo	Siento
Tú	Confiesas	Atiendes	Sientes
Él, ella, usted	Confiesa	Atiende	Siente
Nosotros/as	Confesamos	Atendemos	Sentimos
Vosotros/as	Confesáis	Atendéis	Sentís
Ellos/as, ustedes	Confiesan	Atienden	Sienten

However, there are cases in which a verb meeting these condition will have its "e" weakened instead, becoming "i" rather than "ie". It usually happen with verbs ending on -ir and having the last letters of the root being "gu", "g", or "d".

Persona	Seguir	Regir	Medir
Yo	Sigo	Rijo	Mido
Tú	Sigues	Riges	Mides
Él, ella, usted	Sigue	Rige	Mide
Nosotros/as	Seguimos	Regimos	Medimos
Vosotros/as	Seguid	Regid	Medid
Ellos/as, ustedes	Siguen	Rigen	Miden

If the second to last syllable of the verb has the vowel "o", then it is replaced with "ue".

Persona	Volar	Volver	Dormir
Yo	Vuelo	Vuelvo	Duermo
Tú	Vuelas	Vuelve	Duerme
Él, ella, usted	Vuela	Vuelve	Duerme
Nosotros/as	Volamos	Volvemos	Dormimos
Vosotros/as	Voláis	Volvéis	Dormís
Ellos/as, ustedes	Vuelan	Vuelven	Duermen

If the last letter of the root of a verb is "c", its changed into "zc" only when conjugating the singular first person (Yo).

Persona	Merecer	Florecer	Deducir
Yo	Merezco	Florezco	Deduzco
Tú	Mereces	Floreces	Deduces
Él, ella, usted	Merece	Florece	Deduce
Nosotros/as	Merecemos	Florecemos	Deducimos
Vosotros/as	Merecéis	Florecéis	Deducid
Ellos/as, ustedes	Merecen	Florecen	Deducen

Always be wary of exceptions to the rule. For example, "cocer" (to cook, to boil) has its' root finishing in "c", but its singular first person is conjugated as "cuezo", not "cuezco". The "e" on "suspender" (to suspend, to discontinue) neither weakens nor it has its "e" replaced by "ie", and "conocer" (to know, to meet) doesn't turn its second to last vowel into "ue", it only changes its "c" with a "zc".

While these rules are handy if you need a clue on what to do, the best way to learn those, much like in English, is through memorization. Always have a dictionary at handy when learning verbs, one which contains a conjugation table.

EXERSICES:

Conjugate on Present Indicative the following verbs. Keep in mind some of these verbs might be irregular.

Persona	Transferir	Comer	Conocer	Adoptar
Yo				
Tú				
Él, ella, usted				
Nosotros/as				
Vosotros/as				
Ellos/as, ustedes				

Persona	Plantar	Abrazar	Trabajar	Ayudar
Yo				
Tú				
Él, ella, usted				
Nosotros/as				
Vosotros/as				
Ellos/as, ustedes				

Verbos "Ser" y "Estar" (THE 2 "TO BE" VERBS):

This is a tricky part of learning Spanish but a very important one, considering how commonly "to be" is used in both languages. In Spanish, the verb "To be" is separated into two instances: "Ser" and "Estar".

"Ser" is used when we are talking about characteristics of a noun that are meant to be permanent or long lasting like features, origins, professions, relationships, and time.

El cielo es azul — The sky is blue
El pastel es grande — The cake is big
Este juguete es de China — This toy is from China
Mi sombrero no es de Panamá — My hat is not from Panama
Rafael es médico — Rafael is a physichian
Nina es abogada — Nina is a lawyer
Catrina es mi esposa — Catrina is my wife
Brito es mi novio — Brito is my boyfriend
Carlos es colombiano — Carlos is colombian
Luis es venezolano — Luis is venezuelan

"Estar", on the other hand, is used when talking about something that isn't considered to be temporary. These includes locations, current condition, emotions, physical state and actions. Permanent conditions that are not meant to be appropriate to the object are included as well.

Mi amigo está en la tienda — My friend is at the store
Los niños están en el parque — The kids are at the park
Papá está enfermo — Dad is sick
Mamá está cansada — Mom is tired
El disco está rayado — The disk is scratched

La cuchara está rota — The spoon is broken
Claudia está preocupada — Claudia is worried
Gladys está contenta — Gladys is happy
Lila está jugando conmigo — Lila is playing with me
Guillermo está comprando verduras — Guillermo is buying groceries

Note that there are words that can use for both "Ser" o "Estar" and depending of what you use, the meaning of the word can change completely. That's because some words have multiple meanings. We must remember to make difference between characteristics and conditions in those cases. Having a dictionary at hand also comes in handy.

La manzana es verde — The apple is green [colored]
La manzana está verde — The apple is green [unripe]
Mi cara es roja — My face is red [has a permanent red tone]
Mi cara está roja — My face is red [is blushing out of shame or anger]

Conjugation for the verb "ser" in present tense is as follow:

Yo soy — I am
Tú eres — You are
Usted es — You are (forma)
Él es — He is
Ella es — She is
Nosotros/Nosotras somos — We are
Vosotros/as sois — We are
Ellos/ellas son — They are

This is the conjugation of the verb "estar" in present tense:

Yo estoy — I am
Tú estás — You are

Usted está — You are (formal)
Él está — He is
Ella está — She is
Nosotros/nosotras estamos — We are
Ellos/Ellas están — They are

EXERSICES:

Complete the verb of the following sentences with either "ser" o "estar". Some answers may use both "ser" and "estar" for different results.

Mi perro está enfermo — My dog is sick

El espejo es grande — The mirror is big

La camiseta ___ roja — The T-Shirt is red

El té ___ caliente — The Tea is hot

El profesor ___ adentro — The teacher is inside

Tu gato ___ agresivo — Your cat is agressive

Este sillón ___ azul — This armchair is blue

Mi cama ___ cómoda — My bed is comfortable

El plato ___ roto — The plate is broken

El concierto ___ ruidoso — The concert is noisy

La ayuda ___ en camino — Help is on their way

El paquete ___ pesado — The package is heavy

Lucía ___ apenada — Lucia is embarassed

El Fútbol ___ divertido — Football is fun

El pueblo ___ lejos — The village is far away

El mapa ___ al revés — The map is backwards

El cereal ___ rancio — The cereal is stale

La vaca ___ comiendo — The cow is eating

Él ___ mi primo — He is my cousin

Este colchón ___ duro — This mattress is hard

110

El español ___ fácil — Spanish is easy	Apostar ___ adictivo — Gambling is addicting

Pedro ___ mi novio — Pedro is my boyfriend

Carla ___ acalorada — Carla is hot

Andrés ___ jugando — Andrés is playing

Camila ___ graciosa — Camila is funny

Mi tío ___ inteligente — My uncle is smart

La sopa ___ barata — Soup is cheap

Mi hijo ___ aburrido — My son is boring

Mi hijo ___ aburrido — My son is bored

Mamá ___ tejiendo — Mom is knitting

Nicolás ___ un genio — Nicolás is a genius

___ corriendo — He's running

Lila ___ bonita — Lila is pretty

Papá ___ preocupado — Dad is worried

Pedro ___ mi hermano — Pedro is my brother

Mi tía ___ cansada — My aunt is tired

Mis padres ___ estrictos — My parents are strict

La tabla ___ rota — The plank is broken

Correr es agotador — Running is exhausting

El gato ___ mojado — The cat is wet

Tus amigos ___ raros — Your friends are weird

Paula ___ deprimida — Paula is depressed

Tus retos ___ severos — Your challenges are severe

El vaso ___ está muy alto — The cup is too high

Los árboles ___ verdes — Trees are green

Las rosas ___ rojas — Roses are red

Carlos ___ mareado — Carlos is dizzy

Eso no ___ comida — That is not food

Tu tortuga ___ pintada — Your turtle is painted

El verbo "Hacer" (VERB "TO DO"):

"Hacer" is one of those interesting verbs that gets used around a lot. And as any verb of common use, it is also an irregular verb. Its conjugation is as follows:

Persona	Presente	Pretérito	Imperfecto	Futuro
Yo	Hago	Hice	Hacía	Haré
Tú	Haces	Hiciste	Hacías	Harás
Él, ella, usted	Hace	Hizo	Hacía	Hará
Nosotros/as	Hacemos	Hicimos	Hacíamos	Haremos
Vosotros/as	Hacéis	Hicisteis	Hacíais	Haréis
Ellos/as, ustedes	Hacen	Hicieron	Hacían	Harán

It's main purpose is to be used as the verb "to do" and "to make".

Yo hago el ridículo en clases — I make a fool of myself in class
Tu haces dibujos bonitos — You make awesome drawings
Pablo hace una ensalada — Pablo makes a salad
Mis hermanos hacen una estatua en miniatura — My brothers are making a miniature stature

However, it is also used to measure how much time has passed since the happening of an event up to today. "Hacer" can only be used on countable units of time, it cannot be used on specific dates or events like seasons. It can be used to count how many months has passed or vagues amounts of countable time but not how many instances of an specific month has passed.

Luna saludó a Diego hace una hora — Luna greeted Diego an hour ago

Mamá recibió el paquete hace dos mes — Mom received her package a month ago

Rita ha querido ver esa película desde hace mucho — Rita wanted to see that movie for so long

"Hacer" is also used on weather expressions for temperature or how good it is. This is one of those cases where literal translation makes everything strange, so "It [to be] [weather]" is translated as "[hacer] [clima]".

Hace calor afuera — It is hot outside

Hizo frío en la mañana — It was cold in the morning

Mañana hará buen tiempo — Tomorrow's weather will be nice

El verbo "Tener" (The VERB "TENER" (TO HAVE)):

"Tener" is an irregular verb, it's also one of those that is used very often and doesn't translate as you might expect. It's conjugation is as follows:

Persona	Presente	Pretérito	Imperfecto	Futuro
Yo	Tengo	Tuve	Tenía	Tendré
Tú	Tienes	Tuviste	Tenías	Tendrás
Él, ella, usted	Tiene	Tuvo	Tenía	Tendrá
Nosotros/as	Tenemos	Tuvimos	Teníamos	Tendremos
Vosotros/as	Tenéis	Tuvisteis	Teníais	Tendréis

On its literal translation, we use it when we want to expresses we own something, much like "to have".

Tengo una muñeca vestida de rosa — I have a doll dressed in pink
Hector tiene una bicicleta nueva — Hector has a new bycicle
Liliana tiene un lazo rosado — Liliana has a pink bow
Los amigos de Ricardo tienen un patio enorme — Ricardo's friends have a huge backyard

However, "tener" has many interesting uses outside what you might expect. When paired with "que", its meaning changes from "have to", as in something must be done or needs to be done.

Nuestra tarea tiene que ser original — Our homework has to be original
Las plantas tienen que ser regadas en la mañana — The plants must be watered in the morning

114

Jorge tiene que irse de vuelta a su casa — Jorge has to go back to his house

We also use "Tener" when we are feeling or doing certain something temporary. It's similar to saying "to have fun", except Spanish has its own verb for it (divertir) and there are other sensations we can have but not actually possess, some examples are:

Tener hambre — To be hungry
Tener sueño — To be sleepy
Tener cuidado — To be careful
Tener calor — To be hot
Tener frío — To be cold
Tener miedo — To be afraid

El pez tiene hambre — The fish is hungry
Carlos tiene sueño — Carlos is sleepy
Tengo miedo a las alturas — I'm afraid of heights

El verbo "haber" (THE VERB "TO HAVE" OR "THERE IS"):

"Haber" is an irregular verb in many ways. It's an auxiliary verb that doesn't hold meaning on its own, but it is used when we want to say something was done. It's used on tenses way too advanced for us right now but it's worth mentioning now because of its secondary use.

This verb has an alternate form, "hay". It translates directly as "There are" or "There is" and it's used to signal the existence of something. "Hay" has neither plural nor gender.

Hay una moneda en la mesa — There is a coin in the table
Hay palomas en la plaza — There are pigeons in the plaza
Hay un globo en el árbol — There's a balloon on the tree
Hay osos en el bosque — There are bears in the forest

While it isn't affected by number or gender, it is affected by time. "Hay" is only used in the present, but we also have "había" and "hubo". Both of them mean "There were" and "There was", but each have different applications depending on the situation.

"Había" is considered as preterit, an action that took place in the past and is already done. We use it when we want to say there was a continuous existence of something in the past but it's no longer there.

Había comida en la pajarera — There was feed on the bird house
Había un columpio en este espacio — There was a swing on this space
Había vendedores ambulantes en esta avenida — There were peddlers in this street
Había cocos en la bolsa — There were coconuts on the bag

116

"Hubo" also takes place in the past, but instead of pointing out the existence of something, it let us know an event happened. It is considered imperfect preterit, a tense we'll get to explore later.

Hubo un concierto en el estadio — There was a concert at the stadium

Hubo tres asaltos de demostración de boxeo — There were three boxing demonstration assaults

Hubo una renuión de propietarios hace poco — There was an owner's meeting a bit ago

Hubo cuatro fiestas el mes pasado — There were four parties last month

Lastly, there's "habrá", which is the future form of "haber". We use it on sentences that point out the possibility of something happening or being present.

Habrá un banquete esta noche — There will be a feast tonight

Habrá invitados de honor en la cereminia — There will be honored guests at the ceremony

Habrá una trapesista en el circo — There will be a trapeze artist in the circus

Habrá mulas en el zoológico de contacto — There will be mules at the contact zoo

EXERSICES:

Complete the following sentences using the correct form of the verb "haber". Discern if it should use it's present, preterit, inperfect preterit, or future form.

Hay una serpiente en esas botas — There's a snake on those boots

Hubo un accidente esta mañana — There was an accident this morning

Había mucha gente en el supermercado — There was a lot of people at the supermarket

Habrá un acto de inauguración — There will be a opening act

_____ cangrejos en la playa — There will be crabs at the beach

_____ una cola larga por helado — There was a long queue for ice cream

_____ un pájaro anidando en mi ventana — There is a bird nesting on my window

_____ un lagarto en mi terrario pero escapó — There was a lizard in my terrarium but it escaped

_____ una protesta en la avenida principal — There was a protest on the main street

_____ un puestos de perros calientes aquí — There was a hot dog stand here

_____ normas que debemos seguir — There are rules that we must follow

_____ dos perros cuando me fui — There were two dogs when I left

_____ comida gratis para los primeros en llegar — There will be free food for those who come first

_____ un pez dorado en el tazón — There is a goldfish in the bowl

_____ una tormenta muy grande esta tarde — There was a big storm this afternoon

_____ una cosecha muy grande este otoño — There was a big harvest this autumn

_____ demasiado aceite en la olla — There is too much oil on the cooking pot

_____ personas en taquilla pidiendo reembolso — There were people at box-office asking for refunds

_____ tiempo de sobra cuando lleguemos — There will be plenty of time when we get there

_____ un balancín en buenas condiciones — There is a rocker on good conditions

_____ un perro esperando a su dueño afuera — There was a dog waiting for his owner outside

_____ una batalla de guerra civil en esa colina — There was a civil war battle on that hill

Sujeto tácito (PRONOUN DROPPING):

You might have noticed that Spanish tries its best to cover all possible types of person, number of people, and tense using only verb conjugation. This leads to a phenomenon absent in English but present on many other languages called pronoun dropping.

This happens when the pronoun representing the noun on the sentence is removed from it. This can't be done in English (or at least it shouldn't), dropping pronouns in English could lead to moments in which we would get a sentence we only know if it's directed to a singular third person or not, and it only gets worst when using other tenses.

Walks the dog — It sounds bad and we don't know who walks the dog, it may even be another dog
Walk the dog — Is it me? You? Are we walking the dog or they are the ones walking it?

However, in Spanish such confusion doesn't happen due to how specific verb conjugation is. In fact, there are times when this is necessary in order to sound native. This happens because we already know to which person and how many people the sentence is directed to by only using the verb, putting a pronoun too is not necessary and sometimes it may be excessive.

Paseo al perro — [I] walk the dog
Paseas al perro — [Informal Singular You] walk the dog
Pasea al perro — [He/She/Formal Singular You] walk the dog
Paseamos al perro — [We] walk the dog
Paseáis al perro — [Informal Plural You] walk the dog
Pasean al perro — [They/Formal Singular You] walk the dog

Note that it's not like the pronoun stopped existing inside the sentence, it just became silent for the sake of simplicity. Of course, we can't just drop pronouns out of sentences however we feel like. There are some things to keep in mind first.

The only pronouns we can drop without giving it much thought are "Yo", "Tú", "Usted", "Nosotros" and "Vosotros". Since they are always related to the speaker and the listener, there's no need for them to stay at all. We can still use them in the sentence, but it will give a strong emphasis on the noun doing the action, similar to English when we don't use contractions where normally there would be one.

Soy el más fuerte — I'm the strongest
Tú no es el más fuerte, yo soy el más fuerte — You are not the strongest, I am the strongest

When we talk about third parties, this works a bit differently, if we drop their pronoun out of nowhere it will create confusion. First, we must make sure the person is properly announced, then we can drop their pronoun.

Manuel duerme bajo el sol, da vueltas en la arena al dormir — Manuel sleeps under the sun, [he] rolls in the sand on his sleep

This can be done even when talking about multiple people in third person, all we need to do in order to avoid confusion is to pronoun drop one person at a time during the conversation. If the conversation changes its focus to another third party, then they must be mentioned first, then we can continue dropping pronouns.

Hector es un buen niño, hace toda su tarea sin que lo manden. Carlitos necesita más atención, no puede quedarse quieto en su silla — Hector is a good kid, [he] makes all his homework without telling him. Carlitos needs more atention, [he] can't stand still on his seat

EXERSICES:

Read the next sentences and use the verb to identify the pronoun dropped.

Premian a mi hermano por sus esfuerzos — _____ reward my brother for his efforts

Estoy en una boda en este momento — _____ at a wedding right now

Luchamos por la justicia — _____ fight for justice

Carlos está ocupado, trabaja en una projecto importante — Carlos is busy, _____ is working on an important project

El baile de Madison es hermoso, es la mejor del curso — Madison's dance is beautiful, _____ is the best of the course.

Caminamos por la acera — _____ walk by the sidewalk

Cometes un error — _____ make a mistake

Cambian su televisor por uno nuevo — _____ changed their television for a new one

Arrestaron al criminal más buscado — _____ arrested the most wanted criminal

Servimos la cena cuando está caliente —_____ serve dinner when it's hot

María se perdió, giró en la calle equivocada — María got lost, _____ turned on the wrong street

La hora (TIME):

Time has to be the most frequently asked and explained topic in every language that has ever existed, and now that we have a better understanding of verbs it's a good time to get into it.

First things first. To ask about the time, we simply say:

¿Qué hora es? — What time is it?

To answer that question, we use the structure "Son las [Time]", except when we want to tell it's 1:00. In that case we say "Es la una". For some reason, Spanish considers time not as a noun with a digit, but as a feminine noun (la hora) that increases in numbers from twelve up to twelve.

Son las siete — It's seven o'clock
Son las nueve — It's nine o'clock
Son las tres — It's three o'clock
Es la una — It's one o clock

We can just say the number alone if we want to say it's exactly an specific hour. Still, we can use "en punto" to let know our listener it's exactly that time we're telling.

Son las cuatro en punto — It's four o'clock on the dot
Son las dos en punto — It's exactly two o'clock

Most of the time we'll be talking about time that is not precise, though. For those, it's as easy as adding "y [digit]", that digit being "los minutos" [minutes] past since the hour on the dot. We can also use the preposition "con" instead of "y" if we wish, though "y" is usually preferred. Adding "minutos" at the end is also valid but it's usually avoided in normal conversations as it is cumbersome, its use is limited to radio and automated devices

Son las doce y cinco — It's five past twelve
Son las cinco y veintidos minutos — It's twenty two minutes past five
Es la una con cincuenta minutos — It's ten minutes to two

It's not wrong to say in Spanish that fifty minutes has passed inside an hour, but there are other ways in which we can express the last 29 minutes of an hour. If the minutes are on this half, we can use "Faltan [minutes] para las [next hour]", an expression that translates as It's [minutes] to [next hour]".

Faltan cinco para las doce — It's five to twelve
Faltan veinte para la una — It's twenty to one

When we want to talk about quarters and half an hour, they are expressed as "cuarto" y "media" respectively. They can only be expressed as the examples presented below:

Son las dos y cuarto — It's quarter past two
Son las cuatro y media — It's half past four
Falta un cuarto para las nueve — It's quarter to nine

Great! Now we know how to tell the time according to the clock, but now we need to know how to specify to a person if we are talking about AM hours or PM hours. We can also use a.m. or p.m. if we wish to (they're just written a bit different), but if we want to talk about certain mayor blocks of the day we use four words: "mañana", "tarde", "noche", and "madrugada".

"Mañana" (or "día") talk about the a.m. segment of the day with daylight, "tarde" mentions the p.m. block with daylight, "noche" refers to the p.m. block at night, and "madrugada" is the a.m. block during nighttime, this block can still be called "noche" on its early hours.

Son las tres p.m. — It's three PM
Son las nueve a.m. — It's nine AM
Son las once de la mañana — It's eleven o'clock in the morning
Son las tres de la tarde — It's three o'clock in the afternoon
Son las ocho de la noche — It's eight o'clock in the evening
Son las tres de la madrugada — It's three in the morning

Lastly, there's noon and midnight. For those, we say "Es mediodía" (It's noon) and "Es medianoche" (It's midnight)

EXERSICES:

Now take a pen and rewrite the following times given back into numbers. Leave PM or AM blank if that information is not given.

Son las cuatro y media de la tarde: 4:30 PM

Falta un cuarto para las tres p.m.: 2:45 PM

Es medianoche: 12:00 AM

Son las cinco y cuarenta y dos: 5:42

Es la una de la tarde:

Son las cinco de la mañana:

Son las dos en punto:

Son las nueve y media de la noche:

Es mediodía:

Son las tres con veinte minutos:

Faltan cinco para la medianoche:

Son las cinco con cinco de la mañana:

Son las seis con dos minutos:

Faltan once para las cuatro de la

125

tarde:

Son las dos de la madrugada:

Son las dos y cuarto de la tarde:

Son las siete de la noche:

Son las cuatro en punto:

Son las nueve con doce:

Son las siete de la mañana:

Son las cuatro de la madrugada:

Faltan un cuarto para el mediodía:

Son las dos y media de la madrugada:

Son las doce de la noche:

Son las cinco en punto de la tarde:

Faltan veinte para las tres:

Son las nueve con veinte minutos:

Son las doce y media de la noche:

Es la una con veintiocho de la tarde:

Son las cinco con cincuenta y nueve:

Son las tres con cuarenta y ocho:

Son las dos y media de la tarde:

Son las doce en punto de la tarde:

Faltan veinte para el mediodía:

Son las seis con veintiséis de la tarde:

Es la una en punto de la madrugada:

Son las dos de la noche:

Son las tres y cincuenta y dos:

Faltan quince para las ocho:

Faltan diez para las nueve:

Son las ocho y cincuenta de la noche:

Falta un minuto para la una:

Falta un cuarto para la medianoche:

Son las doce con doce de la tarde:

Son las ocho y cuarenta y dos:

Son las cinco con cuarenta y tres:

Son las siete y media de la tarde:

Son tres con treinta y tres de la tarde:

Faltan diez para el mediodía:

Son las ocho en punto de la noche:

126

Son las nueve y diecisiete de la tarde:	Son las cinco y nueve de la madrugada:
Son las diez y diez minutos del día:	Es la una con un minuto de la tarde:
Son las dos con dos de la madrugada:	Son faltan diez para las nueve:
Faltan cuatr con cuarenta y cinco:	Faltan diez para las tres:
Son las once y treinta y cinco:	Son las ocho y media de la mañana:
Son las siete y once del día:	Son las cuatro con cincuenta y seis:
Faltan seis para las seis:	Son las seis con cincuenta y seis:
Son las once y media de la mañana:	Son las once y cuarto de la noche:
Faltan nueve para las nueve:	Faltan diez para las once:
Faltan doce para las diez:	Son las doce y cuarto de la noche:
Son las diez con treinta y un minutos:	Faltan ocho para las nueve:

Fechas (DATES):

We start learning dates the same way we started learning time: By asking what date is it. for this, we actually have some alternatives:

¿Qué fecha es hoy? — What date is it today?
¿Cual es la fecha de hoy? — What is today's date?
¿A cuanto estamos hoy? — At what date are we today?

For this next segment, we'll need a bit of vocabulary. Here are listed the days of the week and the days of the month. Remember: Days of the week and months are all masculine nouns. Also, months and days of the week are not always capitalized as in English, only if they're the first word on a paragraph.

Days of the week:

Monday — Lunes
Tuesday — Martes
Wednesday — Miercoles
Thursday — Jueves
Friday — Viernes
Saturday — Sábado
Monday — Domingo

Months:

January — Enero
February — Febrero
March — Marzo
April — Abril
May — Mayo
June — Junio
July — Julio
August — Agosto
September — Septiembre
October — Octubre
November — Noviembre
December — Diciembre

When saying dates, we use an structures that names the parts of the date from the lowest time block to the largest:

El [day of the month] de [month] del [year]

This order modifies the way date abbreviation works from one language to the other. In Spanish, it's written as in [Day]/[Month]/[Year]. Also, Spanish speakers do not spell years as English speakers do. While English spell most years into double digits, Spanish speakers name years as a single number no matter the year.

05/05/1962
5 de mayo de 1862 — May 5, 1962
Cinco de mayo de mil novecientos sesenta y dos — May fifth, nineteen sixty-two

09/09/2016

9 de septiembre del 2016 — September 9, 2016
Nueve de septiembre del dos mil dieciseis — September nine, twenty sixteen

03/02/1998
3 de febrero de 1998 — February 3, 1998
Tres de febrero de mil novecientos noventa y ocho — February thrid, nineteen ninety eight

25/12/2018
25 de diciembre del 2018 — December 25, 2018
Veinticinco de diciembre del dos mil dieciocho — December twenty five, twenty eighteen

20/08/2000
20 de agosto del 2000 — August 20, 2001
Veinte de agosto del dos mil — August 20, two thousand and one

You might have noticed the year 1862 uses "de" instead of "del". For this instances , the article "el" is omitted because it's not necessary and placing it there causes a repetition of sounds that get unpleasant both to say and hear, a phenomenon called "cacophony". The correct way to use the articles and prepositions of the years between 1000 and 1999 is to use "de" only, otherwise we use "del".

Whether we should use "del" or "de" behind the year has been a topic of minor controversy since the year 2000, time when the discrepancy came to light. This confusion comes from the fact that people had been using "de" for the last thousand years and a topic this mundane usually isn't touched by popular masses, at least until the arrival of the new millennium. Hopefully this will get cleared up as time passes.

Back to dates in general, if we want to mention a date with its date of the week, we add the day of the week with a coma in front.

Martes, 19 de septiembre del 2017 — Tuesday, September 19, 2017
Jueves, 11 de junio del 2015 — Thursday, June 11, 2015

For years taking place on big segments of human history, we also use abbreviations to communicate we are talking from periods ranging from Before Christ to Anno Domini. They're used the same way, but of course since it's a different language, they look a little different.

B.C. : Before Christ — a.C. : antes de Cristo
A.D. : Anno Domini — d.C. : después de Cristo
BCE : Before the Common Era — AEC : Antes de la era común
CE : Common Era — EC : era común

220 B.C. — 220 a.C.
220 Before Christ — 220 antes de Cristo

We can put any of these dates in a sentence as normal nouns or objects, just keep this in mind: Modifying the days of the week from singular to plural will alter the frequency in which we do an activity. Use singular if it's a single time, and plural if it's an ongoing routine.

Voy el domingo a la iglesia — I'm going this Monday to Church
Voy los domingos a la iglesia — I go on Mondays to Church

El fin de semana tenemos reunión — This weekend we have a reunion
Los fines de semana tenemos reunión — On weekends we have reunions

When talking about dates, they're mentioned using defined

demostrative articles except when mentioning months. Talking about a month with a demonstrative article is incorrect, either defined or undefined. Prepositions such as "para", "a", or "de" are allowed, though.

El 31 de octubre celebramos Halloween — At October 31 we celebrate Halloween
El año 2000 fue una fecha importante para la humanidad — The year 2000 was an important date for humanity
Estamos listos para la semana que viene — We are ready for the incoming week
Marzo llegó en un parpadeo — March got here in a blink
Haremos una reunión en abril — We'll have a meeting in April
Esa tarea es para agosto — That homework os for August

EXERSICES:

Translate to Spanish the following hours given. Write them both in numbers and as they're read.

March 3, 1987
3 de marzo de 1987, tres de marzo de mil novecientos ochenta y siete

April 6, 2010
6 de abril de 2010, seis de abril del dos mil diez

January 21, 1264

_____

September 1, 1934

_____

July 30, 2005

November 11, 1912

August 12, 1545

---

522 B.C.

March 4, 122 A.D.

July 2, 1024

---

543 B.C.

October 21, 1999

June 13, 1604

February 18, 1395

March 3, 1827

November 28, 1498

May 9, 2011

December 15, 2010

July 18, 1169

January 18,1846

October 12, 1554

January 1, 2000

February 14, 1929

July 4, 1229

August 6, 1596

June 16, 1968

May 21, 1882

September 8, 1112

March 2, 1858

November 2, 1600

December 7, 1793

August 3, 1628

March 5, 628 A.D.

April 27, 1575

Infinitivos como sustantivos (INFINITIVES AS NOUNS):

Just like English, if we want to tell someone doing something will have an effect on them, we can use a infinitive verb as a noun to talk about that action.

Infinitive nouns are always masculine and most of the time are singular. They can also be used as objects for prepositions and verbs.

Cantar es divertido — Singing is fun
Pasear es relajante — Strolling is relaxing
Jugar antes de trabajar es mala práctica — Playing before working is bad practice
Correr cambió mi vida — Running changed my life
Recordar es vivir — Remembering/To remembet is living/to live

Gerundio (GERUND):

Gerunds, -ing terminations used to indicate ongoing actions, are also used in Spanish. On regular verbs, The termination -ar is replaced with -ando, -er with -endo, and -ir with -iendo. If the stem of a verb ending with -er or -ir finishes with a vowel, we add 'yendo' instead. As always, be careful when dealing with irregular verbs.

Correr, corriendo — To run, running
Caminar, caminando — To walk, walking
Gruñir, gruñendo — To growl, growling
Crear, creando — To create, creating
Roer, royendo — To gnaw, gnawing
Huir, huyendo — To run away, running away

Reír, riendo — To laugh, laughing
Poder, pudiendo — To be able to, being able to

Similar to English, we use gerund to establish ongoing actions in a sentence. They are also used alongside "Estar".

Lucas está escalando con Frida — Lucas is climbing with Frida
Yo estoy comiendo con Fernando — I'm eating with Fernando
Manuel estaba pensando en Gloria — Manuel was thinking about Gloria
Tú estás distrayendo a la clase — You are distracting the class

Gerunds in Spanish can also be used as adverbs to give more sense, information, and modify the verb.

Oliver pasa su tiempo libre jugando — Oliver passes his free time playing
Erica trabajan en su libro cantando — Erica works on her book

singing

Mi grupo sube la colina sudando — My group go up the hill sweating

Ese pajaro llegó hasta acá volando — That bird got here flying

However, their uses in Spanish doesn't mirror 100% their use in English. When referring to verbs as noun we used their base form instead of their gerund, something you might have noticed when using infinitive nouns.

Beber es refrescante — Drinking is refreshing

Empujar es grosero — Pushing is rude

Bostezar no está permitido — Yawning is not allowed

Hacer pesas es doloroso los primeros días — Lifting is painful the first days

EXERSICES:

Read the following sentences. Mark those that aren't using gerund properly.

[__] Mi papá está leyendo un libro — My dad is reading a book

[__] Protejo mis ojos con lentes de nadando — I protect my eyes with swimming googles

[__] Pedro está de vacaciones — Pedro is on vacation

[__] Mi abuelo está contando una historia — My grandfather is telling a story

[__] Laura está cantando — Laura is singing

[__] Lisa se está peinando — Lisa is brushing her hair

[__] Pedro estaba peleando con Pablo — Pedro was fighting with Pablo

[__] Manuel estaba escalando la montaña — Manuel was climbing the mountain

[__] Nicolás está empunjando a otros niños — Nicolás is pushing other kids

[__] Carmen está paseando — Carmen is walking

[__] José está haciendo la tarea — José is doing his homework

[__] Lucía se está poniendo maquillaje — Lucía is putting on makeup

[__] Rita está cocinando la cena — Rita is cooking diner

[__] Comiendo es mejor que cocinando — Eating is better than cooking

[__] Mis hijos están pidiendo mesada — My children are asking for allowance

[__] Mi sueño se está haciendo realidad — My dream is coming true

[__] Mi teléfono está fallando — My phone is failing

[__] Estoy pagando mis compras — I'm paying for my purchases

[__] Mateo nunca sale sin su casco de cicleando — Mateo nevers leaves without his cycling helmet

[__] Nina está esperando el autobus — Lila is waiting for the bus

[__] Corriendo todos los días es saludable — Running everyday is healthy

[__] El profesor está preparando el examen — Teacher is preparing the test

[__] Frida está estudiando matemática — Frida is studying math

[__] El niño está construyendo una casa de paletas — The kid is building a house out of ice cream sticks

[__] Rubén está cazando venados — Ruben is hunting deers

[__] Mi sobrina sigue queriendo un poni — My niece still wants a pony

[__] Estudiando te hace más culto — Studying makes you more cultured

[__] Jorge se pasa el día nadando — Jorge passes the day swimming

[__] Nuestro tío sigue en el bar tomando cerveza — Our uncle is still at the bar drinking beer

[__] Las niñas se divierten bailando y cantando — Girls have fun dancing and singing

[__] Los estudiantes siguen pensando en inglés — Students are still thinking in english

[__] El perro sigue ladrando a todo el mundo — Dog keeps barking at everybody

[__] Lucas pierde su tiempo y dinero apostando — Lucas loses his time and money gambling

[__] Mamá está tejiendo un suéter — Mom is knitting a sweater

[__] Laila quiere salvar al planeta plantando árboles — Laila wants to save the planet planting trees

[__] Los monos adoran jugar haciendo muecas — Monkeys love to play making faces

[__] Miguel se entrena corriendo — Miguel trains by running

[__] Tu hermano se defiende pateando — Your brother defends himself by kicking

[__] Botando basura está prohibido — Littering is prohibited

[__] Mona estudió viendo videos educativos — Mona studied watching educational videos

[__] Nelson ve mejor el horizonte saltando — Nelson watches the horizon better by jumping

[__] Roger está mejorando sus ventas — Roger is improving his sales

[__] Ana entra a la casa pidiendo permiso — Ana enters the house asking for permission

[__] Mi amigo asustó al perro tomándo una foto — My friend scared the dog taking a photo

[__] Las serpientes resuelven todo mordiendo — Snakes solve everything biting

[__] Nosotros pasamos rápido el tiempo cantando — We pass the time fast singing

[__] Mauricio está jugando videojuegos — Mauricio is playing videogames

[__] Pablo se está estirando — Pablo is stretching

[__] Norma está pensando en qué ponerse — Norma is thinking about what to wear

Tiempo pretérito (PRETERITE TENSE):

Preterite tense is used when we mention actions that took place in the past and has been concluded, beginning and ends of events, specific times something happened, or sequences of events.

Marta comió papas fritas — Marta ate french fries
Vencí a Lucas en ajedrez — I beat Lucas at chess
La venta de verano terminó temprano — Summer sales ended early
Gloria llegó antes de la hora de cierre — Gloria got there before closing time
Fui a dormir a las diez — I went to sleep at ten o'clock
Me levanté a las seis — I got up at six o'clock
Levantaste la cabeza, me miraste y volviste a dormir — You raised your head, looked at me, and went back to sleep
Julia terminó de desayunar, se cepilló y se fue a trabajar — Julia finished her breakfast, brushed her teeth, and went to work

For their conjugation, we remove the termination -ar, -er, or -ir and we replace it with the according person and their corresponding termination. For past tense, -er and -ir share the same conjugation, -ar has its own set of conjugations.

Subject	Verb ending with -ar	Verb ending with -er or -ir
Yo	-é	-í
Tú	-aste	-iste
Él, ella, usted	-ó	-ió
Nosotros	-amos	-imos
Vosotros	-asteis	-isteis
Ellos/as, ustedes	-aron	-ieron

Yo caminé ayer por la playa — I walked yesterday by the beach

Tú miraste a ese perro a los ojos — You looked at that dog in the eyes

Él escaló la montaña fácilmente — He climbed the mountain easily

Nosotros odiamos a la gente engreída — We hate vain people

Vosotros llegasteis a la hora — You made it on time

Ellos marcaron el territorio como suyo — They marked the territory as theirs

Yo accedí a ayudar con la exposición — I agreed to help with the presentation

Tú moliste la pimienta a la perfección — You grinded the pepper to perfection

Élla prometió estar en casa a las diez — She promised to be at home at ten

Nosotros perdimos el rumbo — We lost our tracks

Vosotros metisteis al ratón en su jaula — You put the mouse on its cage

Ellos obedecieron las reglas — They obeyed the rules

Yo fingí estar interesado — I pretended to be interested

Tú expandiste tus horizontes — You expanded your horizons

Usted dirigó al grupo con éxito — You directed the team successfully

Nosotros impartimos buenos modales — We imparted good manners

Vosotros salisteis sin yo notarlo — You went out without me noticing

Ellos sobresalieron en el torneo — They excelled at the tournament

We need to be mindful of stressing when dealing with preterite tense verbs. A common error that leads to lots of confusion is the singular third person form (él, ella, and usted) for verbs ending with -ar, -ó. If the stress isn't properly expressed at the end of the word, it will sound exactly as the singular 1st person of those verbs in present indicative tense, yo. Combining this with pronoun dropping you can completely modify your message without noticing.

[Yo] Camino solo — I walk alone
[Él, ella, usted] Caminó solo — He/She/It walked alone

If you look closely, you'll notice that the conjugation for verbs ending with -ar and -ir for plural 1st person (nosotros) conjugations is the same as in present tense. This is no mistake and it works like that in Spanish. To tell the difference, we must pay attention to context clues in the sentence. That way we know if they're talking about a concluded event in the past or a habit of some sort.

Reparamos computadoras con frecuencia — [We] repair computers frequently
Reparamos computadoras ayer — [We] repared computers yesterday

Traducimos libros como pasatiempo — [We] translate books as a hobby
Traducimos libros hasta la noche — [We] translated books until night

Trabajamos como voluntarios los sábados — [We] work as volunteers on Saturdays
Trabajamos como voluntarios el sábado pasado — [We] worked as volunteers last Saturday

Of course, this applies to regular forms of the verb, it might be different for irregular forms of the verb. The more commonly used, the more likely they're to have an exception. Here's the most common exceptions:

Person	Ser	Ir	Dar	Ver
Yo	Fui	Fui	Di	Vi
Tú	Fuiste	Fuiste	Diste	Viste
Él, ella, usted	Fue	Fue	Dio	Vio
Nosotros/as	Fuimos	Fuimos	Dimos	Vimos
Vosotros/as	Fuisteis	Fuisteis	Disteis	Visteis
Ellos/as, ustedes	Fueron	Fueron	Dieron	Vieron

You're seeing it right, the verbs "ser" and "ir" are conjugated the same exact way. Of course, to identify which one is being used context clues are necessary.

Fui un soldado torpe — I was a clumsy soldier
Fui un hippy cuando era joven — I was a hippy when I was young
Fui al estadio a vender maní — I went to the stadium to sell peanuts
Fui a Francia hace dos años — I went to France two years ago

EXERSICES:

Complete the following sentences by writing its verb conjugated in preterite tense.

_____ (Caminar) toda la avenida — I walked all the avenue

Carlos _____ (Contemplar) el cielo — Carlos contemplated the sky

Papá _____ (Comprar) un regalo para mamá — Dad bought a gift for mom

_____ (Cometer) un error — He made a mistake

Tu jefe _____ (Disfrutar) la comida — Your boss enjoyed the meal

_____ (Hacer) lo que pude — I did my best

Miguel se _____ (Cansar) de esperar — Miguel got tired of waiting

Mis hermanos _____ (Apreciar) tu visita — My brothers appreciated your visit

_____ (Estar) solo con Daniela — I was alone with Daniela

_____ (Tener) mucha hambre anoche — You were very hungry last night

Juliana _____ (Pintar) la casa muy bien — Juliana painted the house very well

Victor _____ (Ser) el ganador del torneo — Victor was the winner of the tournament

La piscina pública se _____ (Llenar) de mosquitos — The public pool was filled with mosquitoes

_____ (Terminar) mi tarea en tiempo récord — I finished my homework on record time

_____ (Nadar) desde la orilla hasta el bote — You swam from the shore to the boat

Esos osos _____ (Ser) un gran problema — Those bears were a big problem

El día de limpieza _____ (Ser) un éxito — Cleaning Day was a success

La policía _____ (Encontrar) el escondite del ladrón — The police found the thief's hideout

_____ (Comprar) una nevera en precio de oferta — I bought a fridge at sales price

Mi traje _____ (Necesitar) una limpieza — My suit needed a cleaning

_____ (Hacer) un excelente trabajo — You did a great job

Mi vieja cámara _____ (Tomar) malas fotos — My old camera took bad photos

Nuestros libros de escuela _____ (Romper) una mesa — Our school books broke a table

_____ (Ir) de paseo a las montañas — We went hiking to the mountains

Belinda _____ (Hacer) muy poco en su casa — Belinda did very little at her home

Nadia _____ (Recibir) una visita sorpresa mía — Nadia received a surprise visit from me

Tiempo pretérito imperfecto
(IMPERFECT PRETERIT TENSE):

This tense is used when we want to talk about abandoned habits, actions that took place in the past but were interrupted, dates of the past, age in the past, or descriptions of people in the past.

Alimentaba al perro cuando sonó el timbre — I was feeding the dog when the bell rang
Corría por el parque todos los días — I used to run through the park everyday
Eran las cinco de la mañana — It was five o'clock in the morning
Mi primo tenía 8 años cuando lo conocí — My cousin was 8 years old when I met him
Mi profesora era más alta que yo hace dos años — My teacher was taller than me two years ago

To use this tense in regular form, we take the termination -ar, -er-, or -ir from the verb and place the corresponding ending. Much like preterite tense, -er and -ir share a conjugation while -ar has one of its own.

Person	Verbs ending with -ar	Verbs ending with -er or -ir
Yo	-aba	-ía
Tú	-abas	-ías
Él, ella, usted	-aba	-ía
Nosotros/as	-ábamos	-íamos
Vosotros/as	-abais	-íais
Ellos/as, ustedes	-aban	-ían

Yo practicaba karate con mi primo — I used to practice karate with my cousin

Tú podabas el césped por dinero — You used to cut the lawn for money

Él odiaba bañarse con agua fría — He used to hate to bath with cold water

Nosotros mirábamos TV hasta la noche — We used to watch TV until night

Vosotros amabais darle besos a la abuela — You used to love giving grandma kisses

Ellos patinaban a diario — They used to skate daily

Yo traía frutas a mamá cada visita — I used to bring fruit to mom each visit

Tú vendías limonada todas las tardes — You used to sell lemonade every afternoon

Ella ofrecía comida a todos sus conocidos — She used to offer food to all her acquaintances.

Nosotros medíamos medio metro menos hace un año — We measured half meter less a year ago

Vosotros mecíais a la bebé cuando tenía sueño — You used to rock the baby girl when she was sleepy

Ellos pretendían ser una pandilla — They used to pretend they were a gang

Yo vivía a dos cuadras de Roberto cuando lo conocí — I lived two squares away of Roberto when I met him

Tú conducías siempre usando el canal equivocado — You used to drive always getting into the wrong rail

Usted huía de mí cuando hablaba de negocios — You used to flee from me when talking about business

Nosotros mentíamos cuando hacíamos algo malo — We used to lie when we did something bad

Vosotros competíais en ajedrez de pequeños — You used to compete

on chess when little
Ellos producían jalea de manzana muy buena — They used to produce very good apple jam

You might have noticed that conjugation for verbs on this tense is the same for singular first and third person. Because of this, in this tense pronoun dropping is also limited for singular first person as it is the case for third person. It still can be used, but context is needed if you want to avoid confusion.

Wrong:
[Yo] levantaba pesas de joven — I used to do lifting on my youth
[Él] levantaba pesas de joven — He used to do lifting on my youth

Right:
Yo era muy atlético, levantaba pesas de joven — I was very atlhletic, [I] used to do lifting on my youth
Él era muy atlético, levantaba pesas de joven — He was very athletic, [he] used to do lifting on his youth

Wrong:
[Yo] ponía cojines ruidosos en los asientos — I used to put whoopee cushions on seats
[Él] ponía cojines ruidosos en los asientos — He used to put whoopee cuchions on seats

Right:
Yo era travieso de pequeño, ponía cojines ruidosos en los asientos — I was naughty as a kid, [I] used to put whoopee cushions on seats
Él era travieso de pequeño, ponía cojines ruidosos en los asientos — He was naughty as a kid, [he] used to put whoopee cushions on seats

As always, be on the lookout for the most commonly used irregular verbs. Here's an example of some of them.

Person	Ser	Ir	Ver
Yo	Era	Iba	Veía
Tú	Eras	Ibas	Veías
Él, ella, usted	Era	Iba	Veía
Nosotros/as	Éramos	Íbamos	Veíamos
Vosotros/as	Érais	Ibais	Veíais
Ellos/as, ustedes	Eran	Iban	Veían

EXERSICES:

Complete the next imperfect tense sentences using the verb given with its proper conjugation.

Yo _____ (Molestar) a mis primos con frecuencia — I used to mess with my cousins constantly

_____ (Estudiar) juntos en la biblioteca — We used to study together in the library

Pámela _____ (Alimentar) a su gato cuando sonó el timbre — Pamela was feeding her cat when the bell rang

_____ (Conocer) a muchas personas interesantes — You used to know interesting people

Nuestros tíos _____ (Viajar) por el mundo en moto — Our uncles used to travel the world in bike

_____ (Ser) las doce en punto cuando fuimos a almorzar — It was twelve o'clock when we went to have lunch

Carla _____ (Tener) el pelo rubio cuando la conocí — Carla had blonde hair when I met her

Eduardo _____ (Tomar) su café sin colar — Eduardo used to drink his coffee without filtering

_____ (Ser) pobres hace unos diez años — We used to be poor ten years ago

La caja _____ (Estar) vacía — The box was empty

Los Núñez _____ (Aspirar) formar una banda — The Nuñez used to aspire to form a band

Yo _____ (Pensar) que los árboles no comían — I used to think trees didn't need to eat

_____ (Cerrar) la puerta cuando tu perro nos saltó encima — We were closing the door when your dog jumped over us

Mi papá me _____ (Llevar) al parque — My dad used to take me to the park

_____ (Tener) la cabeza grande de bebé — You had a big head when you were a baby

Esa señora _____ (Parecer) cansada — That lady seemed tired

El cartero _____ (Entregar) una carta cuando alquien lo llamó — The mailman was delivering an envelope when someone called him

Natalia _____ (Tener) las uñas largas en la fiesta — Natalia had long nails at the party

_____ (Plantar) árboles en su tiempo libre — They planted trees on their free time

Esa mantequilla _____ (Saber) raro — That butter tasted weird

_____ (Ver) la televisión cuando algo hizo ruido en el techo — We were watching T.V. when something made noise on the roof

Yo _____ (Cantar) para el coro de la iglesia cuando vino ese hombre a molestar— I was singing for the church's chorum when that guy came to bother us

EXERCISES:

The following sentences will be either on preterit on imperfect preterit. Differentiate the two as they're presented. Their translation will give you context but not a straight awnser.

Yo estudiaba para ser profesor — I studied to become teacher

Cáterin no sabía cómo atarse los zapatos — Cáterin didn't know how to tie her shoes

Miguel regaló un oso a Angelina — Miguel gave a bear to Angelina

Mis amigos y yo salimos este domingo al cine — My friends and me went this Sunday to the movies

Pedro no pensaba que el sol fuese enorme — Pedro didn't think the sun was huge

Liliana era pelirroja hace unos días — Liliana was red-headed a few days ago

Jugaba en la computadora antes que llegaras — I was playing on the computer before you got here

Transferí mis fondos a tu cuenta — I transfered my funds to your account

Jorge era rubio de bebé — Jorge was blonde when he was a baby

Pablito le temía a la oscuridad — Pablito was scared of the dark

Marta llegó bien a su casa — Marta arrived safely to her house

Diego siempre embestía a sus amigos con afecto — Diego always tackled his friends affectionately

¿Estabas trabajando cuando te llamé? — Where you working when I called you?

Nuestra entrevista estubo horrible — Our interview was awful

La temporada de caza acabó hace unos días — Hunting season ended a few days ago

Alexis se reía cuando veía gente lastimarse — Alexis used to laugh when seeing people getting hurt

Llegamos a la iglesia a las cinco — We got to the church at five

Conocíamos a todas las personas en el vecindario — I knew all the people in our neighborhood

Visitásteis muchos lugares en Lima — You visited many places on Lima

Llegamos antes de las once y media — We made it before half to twelve

Andrea sirvió el almuerzo hace poco — Andrea served lunch a little ago

Tiempo futuro simple (SIMPLE FUTURE TENSE):

This form of future tense may be the simplest but it has plenty of applications. It's used when we want to talk about probabilities, possibilities, suppositions, predictions, conditional sentences and even solemn commands.

Sacaré cara en mi próximo lanzamiento de moneda — I'll get Head on my next coin flip
Robaré un As en mi siguiente turno — I'll draw an Ace on my next turn
El juez encontrará al acusado culpable — The judge will find the accused Guilty
Mañana lloverá todo el día — Tomorrow will rain all day
Saldré contigo si termino temprano la tarea — I'll go out with you if I finish my homework early
No levantarás tu espada contra mí — You shall not raise your sword against me

To get this tense, all we have to do is get the termination according to the person we're talking about and put it at the very end of the verb. For this tense, the whole verb is the root, there's no need to remove -ar-, -er, or -ir.

Persona	Terminación por reemplazar a -ar, -er, o -ir
Yo	-é
Tú	-ás
Él, ella, usted	-á
Nosotros	-emos
Vosotros	-éis
Ellos/as, ustedes	-án

Yo completaré este nivel antes de la cena — I'll finish this level before dinner

Tú cantarás bonito si practicas mucho — You'll sing pretty if you practice a lot

Él comerá después con su novia — He'll eat later with his girlfriend

Nosotros dedicaremos un poema al profesor — We'll dedicate a poem to our teacher

Vosotros saltaréis la cerca apenas voltee la cabeza — You'll jump the fence as soon as I turn my head.

Ellos contratarán a un entrenador — They'll hire a coach

Yo creceré hasta ser más alto que todos — I'll grow up until I'm larger than everyone

Tú prenderás esa pila de hojas en llamas — You'll set that pile of leaves on fire

Ella entenderá nuestro problema — She'll understand our problem

Nosotros daremos lo mejor mañan — We'll give out best tomorrow

Vosotros morderéis el anzuelo si no prestan atención — You'll bite the bait if you don't pay attention

Ellos conocerán el dolor de hacer enojar a mamá — They'll meet the pain of making my mom angry

Yo recibiré halagos por mis regalos — I'll get praises for my gifts

Tú irás conmigo al cine — You'll go with me to the movies

Usted deducirá rápido la solución — You'll deduce quickly the solution

Nosotros dormiremos con la ventana abierta — We'll sleep with our window open

Vosotros repartiréis estas galletas en la escuela — You'll distribute these cookies at school

Ellos escribirán un discurso de bienvenida — They'll write a welcome speech

Irregular forms appear here as well, except they follow some simple rules to make them sound better. For irregular verbs on this tense, there are three categories. We have verbs that drop the "e" on their termination, verbs that replace the "e" or "i" of their termination with a "d", and irregular roots.

Regardless of the special case, all those verbs still use the regular conjugation table. The only thing that is irregular about them is their root.

Verbs ending on -er that drop their "e":

Person	Saber	Querer	Haber
Yo	Sabré	Querré	Habré
Tú	Sabrás	Querrás	Habrás
Él, ella, ustedes	Sabrá	Querrá	Habrá
Nosotros/as,	Sabremos	Querremos	Habremos
Vosotros/as	Sabréis	Querréis	Habréis
Ellos/as, ustedes	Sabrán	Querrán	Habrán

Verbs ending on -er and -ir that replace their "e" or "i" with "d"

Person	Venir	Salir	Tener
Yo	Vendré	Saldré	Tendré
Tú	Vendrás	Saldrás	Tendrás
Él, ella, usted	Vendrá	Saldrá	Tendrá
Nosotros/as	Vendremos	Saldremos	Tendremos
Vosotros/as	Vendréis	Saldréis	Tendréis
Ellos/as, ustedes	Vendrán	Saldrán	Tendrán

There are some verbs of irregular roots have no trick to them and have to be memorized. However, any verb that is composed of those same verbs will share their irregularity with their family.

Person	Hacer	Rehacer	Deshacer
Yo	Haré	Reharé	Desharé
Tú	Harás	Reharás	Desharás
Él, ella, usted	Hará	Rehará	Deshará
Nosotros/as	Haremos	Reharemos	Desharemos
Vosotro/as	Haréis	Reharéis	Desharéis
Ellos/as, ustedes	Harán	Reharán	Desharán

EXERSICES:

Complete the following sentences with the right tense.

Mamá _____ (Estar) lista a las cuatro — Mom will be ready at four [o'clock]

_____ (Ayudar) a mantener el orden — You shall help mantain order

_____ (Comer) en un restaurante esta noche — We will eat at a restaurant tonight

_____ (Entregar) el libro cuando lo lea todo — I'll give back the book when I read all of it

Esta semana _____ (Bajar) el precio del tomate — This week tomato's prices will drop

El cómic _____ (Salir) a la venta en marzo — The comic will be out on march

_____ (Servir) la cena en un momento — I'll serve dinner in a minute

El puente _____ (Colapsar) con tanto peso — The bridge will collapse with that much weight

_____ (Anunciar) los resultados en dos días — We'll announce the results in two days

Este invento _____ (Ser) un éxito comercial — This invention will be a commercial success

Te _____ (Arrepentir) por eso — You will regret doing that

El desfile _____ (Llenar) las calles — The parade will fill the streets

Tu presentación de español _____ (Ser) buena — Your Spanish presentation will be good

Tomás _____ (Ganar) el torneo de Karate — Tomás will win the Karate tournament

Un día _____ (Perder) la timidez — One day you'll lose your shyness

_____ (Comer) demasiado en el festival — You will eat too much at the festival

Ese pollito _____ (Crecer) en una bonita gallina — That chick will grow into a pretty chicken

_____ (Perder) mi borrador antes de usarlo todo — I will lose my eraser before using it all

_____ (Llegar) de vuelta a casa lleno de tierra — I will get back home full of dirt

Mi nueva casa _____ (Ser) la más lujosa — My house will be the most luxurious

Hoy _____ (Disfrazar) a los niños para Carnaval — Today well disguise the kids for Carnival

Ellos _____ (Ser) el mejor equipo de Béisbol jamás visto — They will be the best Baseball team ever seen

Victoria _____ (Tener) pesadillas si ve películas de terror con nosotros — Victoria will have nightmares if she sees horror movies with us

El exámen _____ (Estar) difícil si olvidamos estudiar — The exam will be hard if we forget to study

La carretera _____ (Estar) llena de huecos — The highway will be full of holes

Las baterías _____ (Estar) cargadas para mañana — The batteries will be charged by tomorrow

Hoy solo _____ (Tener) tiempo para estudiar química — Today I'll only have time to study Chemistry

Esos dos _____ (Romper) a la semana — Those two will break up in a week

EXERSICES:

Read the following dialog. Write down all verbs conjugated in simple future tense and any other word or sentence you don't understand.

Jorge, Manuel y la máquina de Goldberg:

Jorge: Hola Manuel, ¿qué haces?

Manuel: Hola Jorge. Estoy armando una máquina de Goldberg.

Jorge: ¿Máquina de Goldberg?, ¿qué es eso?

Manuel: Es un aparato que usa mecanismos complicados para hacer algo tan simple como servir agua o presionar un botón.

Jorge: ¿Y porqué haces eso? Suena tonto.

Manuel: No es tonto, es divertido de ver. Observa, cuando prenda la máquina, una rolinera rodará por este pasaje hasta tocar esa fila de dominós. Después la fila caerá hasta tocar un interruptor que encenderá un ventilador que soplará aire para mover un barco de papel con vela colgado de una cuerda. Al final, el barco chocará con el interruptor de la luz y la encenderá.

Jorge: Sí, es tonto.

Manuel: ¡Que no es tonto!

Jorge: Como sea, todavía tienes un problema. El barco de papel es muy liviano, cuando choque con el interruptor no prenderá la luz, y para probar la máquina tendrás que ordenar todos los dominós otra vez.

Manuel: ¿Tú crees?

Jorge: ¡Claro! Oye, ¿Y si pruebas cada parte por su cuenta y te aseguras que sirva?

Manuel: ¡Oye, esa es buena idea! Que bueno que te interese la máquina.

Jorge: No me interesa, solo está en el medio de la sala y estorba a todo el mundo... Por cierto, debes poner el ventilador en la potencia más alta. Si no lo haces, el barco no tendrá impulso suficiente para encender la luz.

Manuel: Ya... Oye, se me ocurre una idea.

Jorge: ¿Qué idea?

Manuel: ¿Me puedes prestar a tu hámster por un par de horas?

Jorge: ¿Para que quieres a Bigotes?, ¿Piensas meterlo en esta ridícula máquina?

Manuel: ¡Sí! Verás, ahora que estoy viendo bien mi diseño, noto que los dominós no pesan lo suficiente para encender el interruptor del aire. Pero... ¿Y si entreno a tu hámster para que encienda el aire cada vez que se encienda una luz?

Jorge: Bigotes es un hámster, no un perro. Si no puedo controlar donde se hace pipí, mucho menos voy a adiestrarlo para presionar botones... ¿Y para qué quieres hacer la máquina más complicada de lo que es metiendo un animal vivo?

Manuel: ¡Porque esa es la parte divertida! Hacer la máquina supercomplicada de operar para al final verla hacer su trabajo, no importa si es más fácil para mí levantarme y prender la luz yo mismo.

Jorge: Igual no te voy a prestar mi hámster, no le darás a Bigotes hábitos raros.

Manuel: ¡Aburrido!

Jorge: ¡Si yo soy aburrido entonces tú eres un loco! Solo termina rápido, ¿O.K? Si tu mamá ve eso se enojará contigo.

Manuel: No te preocupes, solo le diré que "está limitando mi creatividad" o algo así.

Jorge: Yo que tú no haría eso. Si abusas, te dirá que uses toda tu creatividad encerrado en tu cuarto... Castigado.

Manuel: Uy...

Jorge: Solo apúrate, ¿O.K?

Manuel: ¡Claro, no hay problema!

Jorge: Y me avisas cuando la máquina esté lista, ¿oíste?

Manuel: ¡Así que sí te interesa!

Jorge: No, solo quiero burlarme de ti cuando la uses y falle.

Manuel: Eres demasiado fatalista, Jorge. ¡Te aseguro que mi máquina va a funcionar!

Jorge: Y yo te aseguro que encontrarás una forma de echar esa monstruosidad a perder. ¡Nos vemos!

English translation

In this conversation, we've got Jorge and Manuel, two young boys talking about a overcomplicated machine Manuel is building. His contraption is known as a Goldberg Machine, a pseudo-machine that has a single purpose but only does it after it activates a sequence of chain reactions.

Jorge helps Manuel with his machine giving him tips, not because he cares about the machine, he does it so Manuel can get done with it fast so Manuel's mom doesn't get angry at him for building that thing in the middle of their living room.

This is a normal conversation with a fairly simple topic taking place in the present so plenty of sentences take place in present indicative tense with a brief use of gerund, as we the main topic is an ongoing action. However, the conversation will briefly transition into simple future tense when talking about the functionality of Manuel's invention.

Manuel is making a prediction on how the machine will work once it's done. Jorge is also making his own assumptions as well, he warns Manuel the machine will fail as it is because of factor he didn't think about. This also applies to Jorge's warning about Manuel's mom. Exaggerated or not, it's still a future event, a not confirmed happening yet to come.

Another interesting bit is Jorge's denial about training his hamster as part of the machine. While it isn't quite solemn, "You shall not teach Bigotes weird habits" is still a command, something Jorge does not want to happen. This is said by a kid, so this would be either said dramatically or translated as "You won't teach Bigotes weird habits".

Another interesting bit is this case of linguistic exchange. Jorge and Manuel refer to Bigotes as a "hámster". It is written exactly as in English, except it has a tilde over "a". However, it is pronounced as if the Spanish H is replaced with an English H. This will happen once in a while when using words borrowed from other languages, specially English.

Keep in mind that not all countries do this. Latinamerica does plenty of linguistic exchanges, but some countries, specially Spain, aren't too keen of foreign words. In those cases, while it isn't impossible for it to happen, "hámster" would exactly as written, with a mute Spanish H.

This is assuming they would use that word at all, some people would prefer to use the name "Cobayo" or "Conejillo de índias", which translates to Guinea Pig. This is a bad translation, as guinea pigs are way larger than hamsters, but some will assume they are the same for the sake of a simplistic translation.

Back to the exercise, this conversation has all uses of simple future tense, from predictions to conditional sentences. Remember to write down all those words and sentences you don't understand. That way you can investigate on your own and get better at learning the language.

If you didn't have to write a word you didn't understand, that's great! It means you're doing a good job expanding your vocabulary. If your notes are full of words you don't know, though, don't worry. A big part of learning a new language is getting a hang of the vocabulary.

If you feel you are having problems on this front, try to study with an English Spanish dictionary at hand, that way you can solve your inquires on the spot. Having a book, an app, or the internet itself at hand helps a lot.

A word of advice: Look up the definitions of the word themselves, do not translate them directly using a translation software. The machine will do its best to change a word for what it thinks it's best suited but it is likely to fail or miss the point.

Searching individual words also has an extra benefit: While translating a text gives you a single replacement of words from one language to another, reading the individual definition of each word will give you better insight on the complete meaning held by that word. Most importantly, different regions of the world give different uses to certain words, even if they're neighbors. Specially when it comes to obscene words.

This may be a simple conversation about some kid building a machine, but there's still plenty to learn only in this short conversation.

El verbo "Dar" (VERB "TO GIVE"):

"Dar" is another common irregular verb in Spanish, one that may be a little too irregular in the language. It's conjugation is as follows:

Persona	Presente	Pretérito	Imperfecto	Futuro
Yo	Doy	Di	Daba	Daré
Tú	Das	Diste	Dabas	Darás
Él, ella, usted	Dará	Dio	Daba	Dará
Nosotros/as	Damos	Dimos	Dábamos	Daremos
Vosotros	Dais	Disteis	Dabais	Daréis
Ellos/as, ustedes	Dan	Dieron	Daban	Darán

"Dar" translates directly as "To Give" but that wouldn't make justice of how many possible uses this word has on the language. It's so widely used it replaces a lot of verbs when used in expressions combined with other words. Some of those cases are:

"dar": Its base form. As said before, it translates as "to give".

Mamá dio una galleta a María — Mom gave a cookie to Maria
Juan me dio una moneda vieja — Juan gave me an old coin

"dar con [object]": It translates as "found". This compositions implies we had a meeting with something or someone along the way

Di con Miguel de camino a casa — I found Miguel on my way home
Marcela dio con un billete de 100 en el parque — Marcela found a 100 bill in the park

"dar por [verb]": This combination means "to decide to [verb]" or "to feel like [verb]". It is used when a person makes the decision of doing something out of the blue or on a whim.

Me dio por comer helado de fresa — I felt like eating strawberry ice cream
A Juan le dio por jugar ajedrez — Juan felt like playing chess
A Diana le dio por nadar — Diana felt like swimming

"dar a luz": It translates as "to give birth". Make sure you always give it its preposition "a", otherwise it turns into "dar luz", which translates as "to give light" or "illuminate".

Juliana dio a luz a Guillermo hace unos días — Juliana gave birth to Guillermo some days ago
Nina dará a luz en un par de semana — Nina will give birth in a couple of weeks

Jorge dio luz a Francisco para que leyera — Jorge gave light to Francisco so he could read
Di luz a mi papá mientras reparaba el auto — I gave light to my dad while he repaired the car

"dar de cabeza": It translates as "fall flat on one's head" or "hit one's head".

Pedro se dio de cabeza contra el piso — Pedro fell flat on his head against the floor
Lucas se dio de cabeza contra el aviso — Lucas his his head against the sign

"dar de narices": Is the same as "dar de cabeza", but instead of the head, the face is what gets hit.

Pablo se dio de narices contra el muro — Pablo hit his face against the wall
Sunana dio de narices contra el hielo — Susana fell flat on her face against the ice

"dar lo mismo": It can be translated as "To not make a different" when talking about an event or "to not care" when referring to a person.

En la reunión da lo mismo si vas vestido de azul o negro — At the reunion it makes no difference if you go dressed in blue or black
A Tatiana le da lo mismo si come atún o no — Tatiana doesn't care if she eats tuna or not

"dar a [object] por [adjective]": Used like this it means "to consider someone as something" or "to assume someone is something". We use it when the noun believes a statement about the object to be true.

Pepe te dio por muerto cuando te caíste — Pepe considered you dead when you fell
Doy este tema como cerrado — I consider this topic as closed
Te dimos por gótico cuando te conocimos — We assumed you were goth when we met you

"darse cuenta de": It translates as "to realize". It is used when the noun becomes aware of something they've missed.

Me di cuenta que pintaron la pared — I realized they painted the wall
Luis se dio cuenta de su error — Luis realized his mistake

"dar un paseo": It translates roughly as "to take a walk" when used alone, but it can be used to describe the act of casually having a recreational stroll on a vehicle, as in "to take a ride on something". It can be used on vehicles of easy access like bikes, cars, or even skates; public transportation also counts. Vehicles that require mayor preparation like a planes or rockets can't be used here unless it is somehow possible to have a moment of leisure riding either of those.

Di un paseo por el muelle — I took a walk through the harbor
Samanta da un paseo en moto — Samanta took a bike ride
Héctor dará un paseo en carro con nosotros — Héctor will take a car ride with us
Endrian daba paseos en cohete — Endrian used to take rocket rides (This is only acceptable in Science Fiction)

"dar la [Time]": This is an expression that translates directly as "to strike an hour". It is only used when mentioning a clock hitting one of its digits. Remember that only "la una" is considered a singular noun.

Salimos a la escuela antes que el reloj de las siete — We go to school before the clock strikes seven
Regresamos cuando el reloj da la una — We come back when the clock strikes one

"dar de comer": This compound translates as "to feed". The verb "Alimentar" exists, and it brings the same exact meaning, but a more common and casual way to say "to give someone food" is "dar de comer".

Mamá le dio de comer al bebé — Mom fed the baby
Francisco da de comer a las palomas — Francisco fed the pigeons

"darse prisa": It translates as "to hurry". Most of the time it's employed as an interjection. Still, it can be used when the noun is making haste.

172

¡Date prisa! — [You] Hurry up!
Miguel se dio prisa para no llegar tarde — Miguel hurried up so he wouldn't be late

"darse a conocer": It translates literally as "to make yourself known".

Me di a conocer en mi primer día de trabajo — I made myself known on my first day of work
Jorge se da a conocer como el más competitivo — Jorge makes himself known as the most competitive

EXERSICE:

Read carefully to the following narrative. Make note of the uses of the word "dar" and any word you may not be familiar with.

Mi encuentro con Mota:

Daba un paseo por el parque cuando en el camino di con un cachorro blanco lleno de tierra, estaba apartado en los matorrales y no se movía. Al principio lo di por muerto, pero entonces empezó a chillar y temblar. Temiendo por la vida del pobre, me di prisa de vuelta a mi casa para darle comida y abrigo.

Le di de comer sardinas, no tenía más nada en la despensa pero le dio lo mismo, dio al pescado barato por glorioso y lo devoró antes de darme cuenta. Tras darle calor al perrito con una cobija, le di compañía y me puse a jugar con él. Estaba débil pero era juguetón, se daba de narices en el pasto tratando de dar con mi mano.

Le di una buena mirada y me di cuenta que tenía una placa llena de barro en el cuello. Pensé que sería bueno dar con el dueño pero iban a dar las seis, era muy tarde para buscarlo. Decidí darle hogar en mi casa mientras tanto.

Le di un buen baño para quitarle el sucio, el pequeño quedó tan blanco como la nieve. Se dio de cabeza con mi sofá tratando de atrapar mi mano antes de darse por cansado e irse a dormir. Me di un momento para ver si la placa tenía un número de teléfono. Al ver que sí lo tenía, le di una llamada al número, pero nadie contestó.

Me levanté el domingo siguiente a las siete. Los fines de semana me doy más tiempo para dormir pero el cachorro me saltó encima y no me dejó dormir. Luego de darle de comer, improvisé una correa y lo saqué a dar un paseo cuando el reloj dio las ocho.

El cachorro se dio a conocer entre mis vecinos. Ladraba y saltaba hacia todos los que veía, no para darles un susto, si no para jugar. El paseo debió tomar media hora, pero por jugar con los vecinos llegamos cuando el reloj dio las diez.

Llamé de nuevo al número de la placa, pero sin éxito. Si no podía dar con el dueño, lo mejor era darle hogar al pequeñito. Desde entonces he estado cuidando de él, al menos lo que pensaba era un "él". Después de dar una buena mirada detrás de todo ese pelo descubrí que era hembra.

Quería darle un nombre, pero la placa ya tenía uno, "Mota". Desde entonces, todos los días tenemos la misma rutina: Mota me despierta, le doy de comer, le doy un paseo cuando los vecinos duermen, le doy un baño, me voy a trabajar, regreso a la casa, Mota salta sobre mi porque me extraña, hago cosas de perro con Mota y la dejo dormir cuando dan las seis.

Mota creció como una perra muy saludable y obediente. Me daba luz cuando trabajaba en mi auto, me daba el periódico cuando llegaba a la casa, recostaba su cabeza sobre mi regazo cuando estaba deprimido y me daba ánimos con besos de lengua.

Ella incluso era más cuidadosa que yo. Varias veces había intentado cruzar la calle cuando Mota me da un tirón desde la camiseta, me daba la vuelta para ver qué quería para luego notar un automóvil o una moto dando un giro en el canal equivocado. Me daría contra un vehículo o incluso me daría por muerto si no fuera por mi velluda protectora de blanco.

Eventualmente, Mota dio a luz a seis cachorros blancos y negros que tuvo con el perro de un vecino. Por lindos que fueran, no podía darle cuidado a siete perros, incluso si mi vecino ayudaba, por lo que los dimos en adopción. Me dio mucha tristeza hacerlo pero no tuve otra opción.

Dí los cachorros a varios vecinos. Algunos se quedaron en el vecindario, pero otro fueron dados en adopción a amigos de ellos. De los cinco, solo dos de ellos los damos por perdidos, no sabemos donde están. Aun así, damos mucho cariño a los perritos, aún cuando ya no son responsabilidad nuestra.

Mota sigue dándole luz a mi vida, incluso hoy. Me da dolor ver lo vieja que se está poniendo, trata de jugar como antes pero se da de cabeza tratando de ser energética, ya no tiene el balance que solía tener. Pero eso no importa, lo mejor que puedo hacer es darle los mejores momentos hasta el final.

In this story, a man taking a stroll on the park finds a dirty white puppy and takes care of it. He tries to find her owner but he can't contact them. In the end, he decides to take care of her, letting her grow into a healthy adult.

She also has her own puppies at some point. Unfortunately, her owner has to give them away since he can only take care or her. She brightens the man's life and he gets sad as he notices she's growing old so he decides the best thing to do is to make her as happy as he can.

In the topic of narratives, fables, stories, tales, and so on; since they're all past experiences, they are always narrated in past tense. For this story we're only using present indicative, preterite, and imperfect preterite tenses, but there are many more past tenses in Spanish, most of them still too advanced for us.

Preterite is mainly used for this sort of text, as it expresses a succession of events that has already happened and it's been told to us, but for events that happened in the past but were interrupted we use for a brief moment imperfect preterite.

One great of example of imperfect preterite is at the very beginning. The man was minding his own business when he found an abandoned puppy. Also, when he's about to name Mota, a Spanish word for "Speck", he interrupts his action since the puppy already has a name on its plate.

Present indicative tense is also used, as strange as it may sound, to express the daily routine of Mota and her new owner. The events are still taking place in the past, but since they are describing still ongoing habits, they're written on present indicative tense.

You might have noticed at the very beginning a pronoun dropping right at the start of the story without context within the narrative, which shouldn't be done in imperfect preterite. It may not look like it to some people but the context is already there.

The title of the tale is "Mi encuentro con Mota", as in "My encounter with Mota". The title alone tells us this is going to be a story narrated from the perspective of the teller, so it's told in first person. Since at that moment the only character in the story is the narrator, it is safe to assume he's talking about himself.

Even without the title, context is given right again when the speaker uses the verb "dar" in first person. This is bad practice and it shouldn't be done, but be aware that it can still happen, even among native Spanish speakers.

On a side note, using the same word over and over on the same conversation without synonyms of any kind is also bad practice. The constant reuse creates a cacophony at larger scale, which makes the text unpleasant. Here we're using "dar" multiple times only as an example of the many applications it has, actually using the verb this much without variation will tire your listener very quickly.

As for the exercise itself, all of the uses presented for the verb "dar" has been presented on the story, from it's simplest form as the verb "to give" to others more curious as it shows its ability to pass as other verbal uses such as "to realize" and "to give birth". Some idiomatic forms of "dar" are present too, like "darse de cabeza/narices" and "darse a conocer".

Remember to also write down anything you don't understand so you can investigate it later.

Spanish Short Stories

This last part of the book has been designed with the purpose of being simple to understand and help the reader to understand the language in a slightly more attractive way.

Likewise, some words that could be difficult are marked with their respective translation into English for your convenience.

In any case, in case you do not know some words, it is always good to have a dictionary at hand to support the studies and better understand the stories.

(Una vez comprendas el idioma español, serás capaz de leer todo esto sin equivocarte ni una vez. Comprenderás a la perfección que es lo que estas historias sencillas quieren enseñarte, o quizá, comprendas que no hay una moraleja en todo. ¡Disfruta y aprende!)

Historia #1: Minerva el caballero.

Mi nombre es Minerva, y siempre he soñado con ser un gran caballero cuando crezca. Por eso mismo he decidido servir a uno como su escudero, pero el caballero al que sirvo, no es como lo que yo sueño ser.

– Minerva, ¿Que tal esta tu día? – Me pregunta.

Él no suele salir en misiones, tampoco cuidar la ciudad. Solamente pasa tiempo el tiempo sentado. Mirando los alrededores, y hablando conmigo.

No pude elegir a alguien más, nadie me hubiera aceptado, pero él se ofreció voluntariamente para tomarme como su escudero.

No suelo verlo junto a su caballo, tampoco hablar con otros caballeros, pasa la mayor parte de su tiempo sentado mirando a los demás pasar. Nunca me he animado a preguntarle que está haciendo, debe ser algo que yo no comprendería, quizá un tipo de misión de caballero de la cual no puede hablar.

Pero no es como el caballero que yo quiero llegar a ser.

Yo quiero llegar a ser un caballero alto y fuerte, que porte la armadura más pesada y reluciente; un símbolo de alguien de la alta clase; una persona que imponga respeto ante los demás; que cuando cabalga, el galope de su caballo retumbe en los oídos de los malos.

*(Spanish Word meaning. **Cabalgar = Ride. Retumbar = Resounds**)*

– ¿Que es una persona mala para ti? – Me preguntó una vez cuando le dije que era lo que quería hacer.

No tenía una respuesta para ello, nunca lo había pensado del todo.

– ¿Alguien que golpea a su mamá? – Respondí.

Mi madre es lo que más amo en el mundo. Desde pequeño siempre me ha tratado bien y ha mirado por mí. Siempre me cuida y me da todo lo que necesito, por eso siento que una persona mala es aquella que maltrata a su madre. Si, a esas personas es a las que quiero derrotar.

– Pienso lo mismo. – Me respondió. – A una madre debes ayudarla en todo. Siempre estar a su lado y demostrarle mucho cariño. –

Eso ya lo hacía desde antes de que me lo dijera.

Siempre he intentado ser agradecido con mi madre, por lo que ayudo en todo lo que puedo.

– Pero no solo basta con ser amable con tu madre. – Recalcó.

– ¿No? – Pregunté.

– Debes ser amable con todo aquel que necesite ayuda. – Respondió.

– Una persona buena ayuda a quien necesita ayuda. –

– ¡Yo hago eso! – Grité con emoción.

Realmente lo hago.

– A veces veo personas en problemas y corro a ayudarlos. Por ejemplo, el otro día, una señora estaba teniendo problemas para levantar unas cosas que habían caído al suelo. Entonces, corrí y la ayude a levantarlas; la señora me sonrió amablemente, me dio acaricio el cabello y me agradeció. – Le dije. – También un anciano el otro día estaba intentando cruzar la calle, pero parecía como que su vista ya no era tan buena, así que lo tome de la mano y lo lleve al otro lado. No estaba muy contento, pero aun así me agradeció algo molesto. –

Aunque después se dio media vuelta y se acercó a mí, dudo un poco, dio un par de vueltas y después susurró algo. No lo entendí, pero aquello parecía avergonzarlo. Rascó su cabeza y volvió a tomar su camino.

– Entonces podemos decir que eres una persona amable. – Dijo el caballero dándome una sonrisa.

Siempre me hace preguntas extrañas; siempre las respondo. No entiendo por qué lo hace, pero tampoco me molesta. Me agrada estar con él, aun cuando no me hace trabajar como debería.

Su armadura siempre esta reluciente, y el siempre saludando a todos los que pasan. Nunca se mueve de su lugar, siempre en el mismo sitio.

– Sabes, no soy muy valiente. – Me dijo una vez. – Le temo a las cucarachas. –

(Spanish Word meaning. **Cucaracha = Cockroach***)*

– ¿En serio? – Le pregunté sorprendido.

Para mí, un caballero debía ser valiente. No podía creer que el caballero al que servia, era alguien que se asustaba con una simple cucaracha.

Mi madre les teme a las cucarachas, por eso sobrellevo mi temor a ellas… no, ¡lo superé!

Cuando estamos en casa, algunas veces aparece una, y ella suelta un grito asustada; rápido corro a donde se encuentra y me encargo de deshacérseme de la cucaracha. Ahí mi madre me mira con orgullo, orgullo de criar un hijo tan valiente. Me da un abrazo y un cumplido por mi acción.

– ¡Yo no les temo en lo absoluto! – Le presumí con orgullo. – ¡Un gran caballero no debe temer ni a los feroces dragones! –

– Pero aquí no existen dragones. – Me dijo el caballero confundido.

No pude contener mi risa.

Incluso él siendo un caballero no estaba al tanto de lo que sucedía.

– ¡Claro que existen! – Dije lleno de confianza. – ¡Solo que no los han encontrado! –

Y para cuando ellos llegaran, yo ya sería un caballero completo.

Sería alto, fuerte y lleno de confianza. Ni una cucaracha más grande podría conmigo.

– A veces me pregunto si en verdad usted es un caballero. – Le dije.

– ¿Por qué lo dudas? – Me preguntó.

Le dije todo lo que pensaba; que él no hacía nada más que estar ahí sentado, mirando a la gente pasar. No salía en misiones, ni parecía ayudar a la gente.

– ¿Qué es un caballero para ti? – Me preguntó por primera vez.

Eso yo lo tenía en claro.

– ¡Alguien bueno! – Ese era el primer punto.

– ¿Cómo alguien que ayuda a su mamá? – Preguntó.

– ¡SI! –

– ¿Qué más? – Preguntó.

– ¡Alguien amable! – Respondí.

– ¿Cómo alguien que ayuda a los ancianos a cruzar la calle? – Preguntó.

– ¡Eso mismo! ¡Así de amables! – Respondí.

– ¿Qué hay de ser valiente? – Preguntó.

– ¡Esa es la parte esencial! – Respondí. – Un caballero sin valor, no es un caballero. Un caballero debe ser sobre todo valiente, hacer frente a los malos sin tener ni una pizca de temor, enfrentarse a las bestias que todos demás temen. Eso es un caballero. –

– Entonces, ¿Eso es un caballero para ti? – Preguntó. – ¿Qué hay de la armadura y el caballo? –

– Cierto, cierto. – Le respondí. – Pero eso viene después. –

– Entonces… ¿No crees que alguien ya es un caballero? – Me preguntó.

El caballero siempre me hace preguntas extrañas, y no las suelo entender del todo. No sé si lo hace solo para seguir hablando conmigo o para distraerse. Quizá es parte de un tipo de entrenamiento. Realmente no tengo la menor idea.

Pero esta vez, siento como si en verdad lo hubiera entendido. No me queda más que darle una sonrisa y responderle.

– Usted solo tiene la armadura, no lo he visto cabalgar. – Respondí.

Aun si parece un caballero, comienzo a dudar de si en verdad lo es.

– Menos mal para caballero no necesita ser muy inteligente. – Me dice. No lo entiendo para nada. – Se está haciendo tarde, deberías volver a tu casa. –

¿Ser inteligente? Es una característica que no había pensado… ¿Un caballero debe ser inteligente?

Como sea, esa es una pregunta para mañana.

– Solo espere un poco más, y verá como seré un gran caballero. – Le digo al señor.

Me despido con una sonrisa, y otro día de trabajo acaba. Siento que cada vez me acerco más a mi sueño.

Historia #2: Un sueño de amor.

Cuando era pequeño me enamore de una niña, aunque en ese entonces no entendía lo que es el amor o amar a alguien en sí. Teníamos mucho en común, ambos teníamos la misma edad, nacimos en la misma ciudad, jugábamos en el mismo parque y... ambos estábamos solos. No es que no tuviésemos padres, a lo que me refería con solos, era que ninguno de los dos teníamos amigos. La verdad es que no entendía el por qué ella jugaba sola, en mi caso, yo era alguien muy tímido como para hablar con los demás, lo cual me hizo estar alejado.

Cuando llegaba al parque ella ya estaba ahí, siempre volteaba, me miraba y me sonreía, a su sonrisa le faltaban dientes, pero... era tan linda. Por alguna razón me sentía feliz de mirarla ahí cada día, aunque no hablásemos sentía que estábamos juntos, aun sin hablar sentía que conversábamos por medio de miradas. Así pasamos un buen tiempo y poco a poco se volvió una rutina.

Recuerdo cuando comenzamos a hablar. Un día llegue más temprano de lo usual, quería mirarla llegar y yo recibirla con una sonrisa, pase horas esperándola, pero no llegaba, estaba ahí... nuevamente solo.

– ¿No te sientes triste? –

Voltee hacia atrás y ella estaba parada detrás de mí. No supe cómo responder, me había tomado por sorpresa.

– Yo si me sentía triste – Dijo. – Pero entonces llegaste y todo cambio –

Mientras yo estaba nervioso, ella hablaba tan fluido como si fuésemos amigos de mucho tiempo.

– Quizá nunca hablamos, pero siento que somos muy cercanos –

– Y-yo me siento igual – respondí tartamudeando.

Aparte mi mirada por la pena de haber dicho tal cosa, cuando voltee a mirarla de nuevo, estaba sonriendo.

– Me llamo María – dijo.

– Yo Daniel – respondí.

– Entonces serás Dany –

Con esas palabras y una sonrisa, una larga amistad inicio.

María era… hermosa, tenía unos bellos ojos verdes como esmeraldas y una piel blanca como la nieve, aun faltándole dientes, su sonrisa era linda, desbordaba confianza con su actitud y forma de actuar, siempre era la que dirigía en todo, eso es lo que más me gustaba de ella.

*(Spanish Word meaning: **Desbordar = Overflow**)*

Gracias a ella poco a poco perdí mi timidez, al menos con ella. Los días pasaban volando estando a su lado, seguíamos jugando en el parque, pero ya no solos, estábamos juntos. Si no jugábamos en el parque estábamos jugando en algún otro lugar; cuando uno no podía salir, el otro iba a su casa. En ocasiones se hacía tarde y pasábamos la noche en casa de alguno de los dos, aun siendo de sexos opuestos, nuestros padres no tenían problemas en que pasáramos la noche en el mismo cuarto o en la misma cama, no era porque éramos unos niños, si no que ellos nos tenían confianza. Y también influía mucho el cariño que mi madre le había tomado a María.

– ¡Que niña tan linda! – decía siempre que la miraba, seguido corría a

186

abrazarla y hacerle cariños. Le había tomado mucho cariño, tanto que en ocasiones solía tratarla mejor que a mí, le preparaba su comida favorita y le daba regalos, aunque en realidad no me molestaba.

Todo hubiese seguido igual, pero mi madre mencionó algo que me confundió.

– Entonces, ¿Qué siente mi pequeño por esa linda niña? –

Habíamos pasado mucho tiempo juntos y cada día nos hacíamos más unidos, pero nunca me había preguntado qué era lo que sentía por ella.

– No te entiendo, nada, supongo – respondí.

– ¿Acaso no te pones feliz cuando estas con ella? – preguntó.

– P-pues sí, pero ¿Eso que importa? Me divierto jugando con ella. – le respondí

Mi madre me miró fijamente como si estuviese enojada, me comencé a preocupar, pero entonces sonrió.

– Después de todo solo eres un niño, no sabes que es el amor –

Era cierto, no entendía nada de eso que llamaban amor, eso de lo que todos hablaban y a la vez discutían que es en realidad. Yo solo quería pasar mis días con ella, así como lo habíamos estado haciendo desde hace ya tiempo… pero eso no era posible.

Un día jugábamos cerca de casa, como era usual, nada fuera de lo normal reíamos como a siempre, seguíamos lo que se había convertido en una rutina para nosotros. Entonces de pronto María se detuvo.

– Sabes Dany… quiero pasar mi vida contigo – Dijo.

No entendía bien a que se refería o a que venía tales palabras, simplemente estaba fuera de contexto.

(Spanish Word Meaning: **Contexto = Context***)*

– Pero algún día creceremos y tomaremos caminos separados, tu encontraras a alguien que te guste y formaras una familia – Decía. – Y no quisiera que pasase eso, me divierto jugando contigo, lo supe cuando te mire por primera vez, el solo hecho de que estuvieses ahí me hacía sentir bien, sentía que estabas conmigo… aun sin hablar. – Yo me sentía de la misma manera, cuando ella llego a mi vida olvide el hecho de que no tenía amigos y cada día me hacía sentir mejor. Cuando me sentía triste lo que más me reconfortaba eran sus cálidos brazos que me rodeaban y sus palabras de aliento, un "Todo estará bien" bastaba para tranquilizarme y hacerme sentir mejor… pero no podía decírselo.

– Así que… estemos…juntos…mientras… podamos... –

Su voz se hacía más baja y los tiempos entre palabras más largos. Eso fue lo último que dijo antes de caer al suelo frente a mis ojos.

Me quede un momento sin comprender que era lo que sucedía, estaba ahí, en el suelo, inmóvil, como si estuviese dormida, pero su respiración se hacía cada vez más rápida. Entonces reaccione, no dude en lo que haría, con las pocas fuerzas de un niño de nueve años la intente subir a mi espalda, pero no era suficiente, me empecé a desesperar, no podía alzarla y era demasiado peligroso dejarla ahí sola, así que en un golpe de adrenalina logre alzarla en mis brazos, corrí los mas que pude intentando no dejarla caer a mi casa, entonces mi madre me miro, llegue con la cara pálida y lleno de tierra.

Llevaron al hospital a María, no sabían que era lo que había pasado,

188

su vida no corría peligro, su respiración había vuelto a la normalidad y solo estaba "Durmiendo". Le rogué a mi madre para que me dejara estar ahí hasta que despertara, no lo dudo ni un poco.

– Mas te vale recibirla con una sonrisa – Me dijo.

Me quede a su lado todo el día y la noche, no despertó. Al día siguiente fue mi madre, me trajo algo de comida y no me pidió volver, no era que no le importará, si no que sabía que esto era importante para mí.

Así pasaron dos días, los cuales se convirtieron en tres y posteriormente en una semana. Estuve a su lado en todo momento, solo iba al baño y cuando comía lo hacía a su lado, le hablaba a diario, intentando hacerla despertar, pero nada funcionaba. A mitad de la segunda semana me derrumbé, tenía miedo, miedo de que no despertara, de que no pudiese estar con ella nuevamente, tantas cosas que no hicimos… tantas cosas que no le dije…

– Vamos María, no me hagas esto, no me abandones, dijiste que querías pasar tu vida conmigo ¿y ahora me dejas? – Le dije – Despierta que tenemos muchas cosas que jugar y cosas que platicar, ya has dormido lo suficiente... así que despierta por favor… –

Me ganó el sentimiento y me eche llorar, no sé cuánto tiempo dure de esa forma, pero seguí hasta que me quede dormido.

Se cumplieron dos semanas y la espera acabo, despertó como si solo hubiese tomado una siesta, no pude llorar de alegría, ya estaba seco, solo, me recibió con una sonrisa y un "Gracias por esperarme". Después de eso pensé que nuestra vida volvería a ser lo de antes y que era el momento de decirle que yo también quería pasar mi vida con ella, después de todo, ya estaba todo bien. No pude estar as equivocado, después de que despertó paso unos días más en el hospital, pero ya no podía seguir ahí, por más que quise no me dejaron "Has hecho suficiente" me dijeron.

Fue irónico que cuando volvió a casa no era un hola, si no un adiós. Debido a que no sabían que había pasado con ella o que lo había provocado, querían ir a una ciudad más grande, donde pudiese estar más segura y con hospitales preparados para cualquier emergencia, después de todo sus padres también se preocupaban por ella.

– Me iré de la ciudad –

Con esas palabras me destrozo, mis planes de pasar mi vida con ella se habían deshecho, no tenía el valor para decírselo ahora que estaría lejos, no sabía que podría pasar mientras no estuviésemos juntos, como ella dijo, quizá en un momento se podría enamorar y hacer su familia, así que desistí en decírselo.

– Así que es un adiós… – Le dije.

Me miro con tristeza, como si estuviese esperando algo más, en verdad no quería irse, le dolía alejarse de mí y a mi igual, pero no podía mostrárselo, solo haría más dolorosa la partida.

– Volveré… – Dijo en voz baja.

Se escuchaba como si lo dijera para sí misma, como si se intentara hacer a la idea o imponerse la meta de volver.

– ¡Volveré! – Gritó– así que espérame por favor, aun quiero pasar mi vida contigo, aunque no haya algo que te atenga a mí, espérame, solo espera a que vuelva y escuchare tu respuesta – Dijo con una mirada decidida.

No podía contestar de la misma manera, aunque yo sentía lo mismo, más me dolía el hecho de que estaríamos separados, así que no di una respuesta… y ella se marchó.

Después de tanto tiempo juntos fue una despedida muy insatisfactoria, me apenaba de haber actuado de tal manera solo para no salir herido, aunque a la larga sería más doloroso lo que había hecho. Así pasaron los meses y me había hecho a la idea de que nuestra historia había terminado, cuando llego una carta, tenía una dirección que desconocía y no parecía ser de alguna empresa o deuda, añadiendo que estaba dirigida hacia mí. La abrí y me llevé una sorpresa, era una carta de María.

*(Spanish Word meaning: **Insatisfactorio = Unsatisfactory**)*

"No creo poder esperar el tiempo necesario para reencontrarnos, así que, aunque sea poco, quiero seguir en contacto contigo, no me diste una respuesta antes y quizá no lo hagas ahora, pero cuando llegue el momento, sea cual sea, la aceptare, por favor, no perdamos esta amistad."

Me sentía bien y mal a la vez, bien por el hecho de que le seguía importando aun habiendo pasado el tiempo y mal por todo lo que había hecho. Aun así, me armé de valor y escribí una respuesta.

Con el tiempo recibí más cartas, leí todas y cada una.

"Se que no ha pasado mucho tiempo, pero ¿Cómo has estado? Yo sigo igual, no he hecho muchos amigos en mi nueva escuela y no pienso hacerlos, la verdad es que no me agradan mucho, prefiero seguir leyendo lo que me envías, sigo esperando la respuesta a lo del otro día."

Después de la primera carta no menciono más sobre que esperaba mi respuesta, no entendía si era porque se le había olvidado o había perdido importancia, pero al leer las cartas que llegaban mis dudas se iban, aunque no lo mencionara, se notaba que esperaba el momento para volver.

Intente no responder de una forma igual a la suya, quería ser un poco más frio para no decepcionarme después… pero no pude, no podía evitar sentirme alegre cada que recibía una carta y esa necesidad de contestarle apenas acabara de leer. Me imbuía con su alegría haciendo que sonriera con cada palabra y riera con su mala forma de explicar las cosas.

Reír, llorar, preocuparme, se volvió una rutina durante los siguientes años, las cartas llegaban casi a diario y en cada una de ellas hablábamos de algo diferente. Mandábamos cartas tan seguido que no daba tiempo a que la respuesta llegase, por eso mismo las conversaciones eran diferentes, habíamos puesto hasta un sistema para diferencias de que trataría la carta.

Así llego en mi graduación de preparatoria una carta diferente, no parecía tratar sobre alguna conversación en particular, no decía nada, a decir verdad, así que con mucha curiosidad me dispuse a leerla.

"Felicidades por tu graduación, ya eres alguien mayor"

Iniciaba con cosas muy básicas y seguía igual, solo me felicitaba por el hecho de haber acabado la preparatoria, nada fuera de lo normal la verdad. Pero eso bastaba para hacerme sentir especial, sus palabras, aunque simples estaban llenas de alegría, en verdad se sentía feliz por mis logros, parecía hasta estar más feliz que yo con ello. Mi sonrisa se hizo más grande al leer la parte final de la carta, en un pequeño apartado, que casi no se miraba y parecía no tener importancia decía: "Volveré pronto". Habían pasado muchos años desde que nos habíamos visto y solo seguíamos en contacto gracias a esas cartas "¿habrá crecido?", "¿Seguirá siendo tan linda?", "¿O se habrá descuidado?" eran unas de las preguntas que invadían mi mente, aunque en realidad no me importaba como estuviese ahora, solo quería mirarla de nuevo, decidí que era el momento, le diría que quiero pasar mi vida con ella, que me sentía mal de no haberlo dicho en el momento, que todo este tiempo fui yo el que más la extrañe aunque no había dicho nada. "Lo haré todo cuando vuelva" pensaba. Mire mi calendario a diario, mirando los días pasar para su llegada, aunque nunca menciono una fecha, lo cual solo me impacientaba más, tomaba en cuenta el tiempo que había pasado desde que envió la carta y llego a mí y el tiempo que llevaba desplazarse de su ciudad a la mía, hacia todo tipo de cálculos solo para saber cuándo llegaría, aunque nada estaba claro, podría pasar un largo tiempo y no la vería, pero ella había dicho "Volveré pronto" y era suficiente para mí.

Entonces pasaron días, semanas… meses. Inicie mi vida universitaria y no podía dejar de pensar en ella, aun habiendo pasado meses no perdía la esperanza, aunque no había notado que no llegaban nuevas cartas, "Debe ser una sorpresa" pensaba, luego fueron dos meses, tres y seguía esperándola con una sonrisa. Se cumplió un año y… nada. Comencé a dudar sobre lo que había dicho, "quizá… cambio de opinión y no volverá, pero no tuvo el valor para decírmelo, quizá… se enamoró de alguien más y se olvidó de mi". Mi felicidad se convirtió en tristeza, me había hecho a la idea de que la esperaría, pero… no había contestado mis cartas ni enviado una después de ese día, al parecer, nuestra historia ahora si había acabado.

Un día cuando volví a casa miré a mi madre de rodillas en el suelo llorando.

– ¿Qué pasa mamá? ¿Por qué lloras? – Le pregunté.

En su mano sostenía un sobre abierto, supe que lloraba por lo que contenía, era una carta, la dirección era la misma que la de María. Supe que era lo que sucedía al momento de mirar la dirección, pero no quería aceptarlo.

"No hay esperanza, no despierta, no queremos verla sufrir más."

Estaba ahí de pie, derramando lagrimas sin saber el porqué, bien podía referirse a otra persona, no necesariamente a ella, pero simplemente no me podía engañar, sabía que algo le había pasado a María, mirar a mi madre en el suelo llorando lo confirmaba, no había duda.

– Tienes que ir Dany – Dijo mi madre. – No la puedes abandonar así, la última vez que paso estuviste con ella y despertó, quizá está esperando que la recibas nuevamente a su lado, así que ve por favor – Aun habiendo pasado años, mi madre le guardaba un gran cariño a María, decía cosas sin sentido, como que ella me necesitaba, aun sabiendo que nada cambiaria con mi presencia, pero estaba destrozada, simplemente quería que yo pasase con ella sus últimos días… que no la dejara sola.

Tuve miedo en esos momentos, me sentí como cuando era un niño, ese temor a amar a alguien que se alejaría aún más de mí, no quería sufrir, no quería verla en tal estado, no quería que me abandonara, así que dude.

–Vete… ¡Vete! – me grito mi madre, estaba realmente molesta. – No quiero volver a verte en esta casa con ese feo rostro, no vuelvas, yo no te necesito… pero ella si –

Aunque fuese solo momentáneo y en el camino se fuese, sentí un valor que me hizo moverme, tome el dinero necesario para ir a su ciudad y tome el primer autobús que salió. Aunque no pudiese cambiar nada, pasaría sus últimos momentos con ella.

El viaje fue largo y apenas bajé del autobús comencé a temblar, tenía miedo de lo que me esperaba, sabía que no sería una imagen agradable. Tomé un taxi al hospital donde la tenían y pedí información en recepción. Me dirigí a su cuarto y fuera de él estaban sus padres, su madre no dejaba de llorar y su padre tenía una mirada seria, intentando parecer duro, cuando por dentro estaba llorando como un niño pequeño.

– Eres tú Daniel… viniste – Dijo su madre limpiándose las lágrimas.
– Pero me temo que es muy tarde, no podemos hacer nada más. –

Comenzó a llorar nuevamente y su esposo la abrazo fuertemente, fue ahí cuando el no pudo contenerse más y comenzó a llorar fuertemente, su llanto se escuchaba en todo el hospital.

Al entrar a la habitación ella estaba ahí… seguía siendo tan bella, su piel era blanca como la nieve, pero ya no podía mirar sus bellos ojos verdes como esmeraldas. La piel estaba pegada a sus huesos, su cara algo demacrada, no podía comer bien en su estado, lo que la llevo a tal estado.

*(Spanish Word meaning: **Demacrada = Emaciated**)*

– M-María… soy yo, sé que quizá no me escuches… pero estoy aquí… a tu lado – No sabía que decirle, a la hora de la verdad simplemente no tenía palabras. Me quede de pie junto a ella mirando tal imagen, esa niña que se robó mi corazón se lo iba a llevar a un lugar aún más lejano que la primera vez.

– María, por favor, te estoy hablando… escúchame… por favor. – Dije. – Te estuve esperando… todo este tiempo, esperando a que volviera y poder darte una respuesta –

Era inútil, no me escuchaba, no había reacción.

– Yo también María… yo también quiero pasar mi vida junto a ti, así que por favor despierta, no me abandones así, no te alejes más de mí, no vayas a un lugar en el cual no pueda alcanzarte, dijiste que volverías y no fue así… incluso vine a buscarte, así que despierta. –

Nada cambiaba, estaba ahí dormida plácidamente, recordé la vez que paso de niños, en solo dos semanas despertó, pero… ¿Cuánto había pasado ahora? Fui ahí sin saber nada, con la esperanza de cambiarlo todo. Entonces entraron sus padres y un doctor.

– Es hora – Dijeron.

Sus padres se echaron a llorar sobre María.

– ¡Perdónanos por favor María! Pero ya no queremos verte sufrir, nos duele mucho, mucho en verdad, pero… esto es lo mejor – Decían.

No comprendía, ¿verla sufrir? No había leído la carta completa, por lo cual no sabía cuánto tiempo llevaba ahí y comencé a decir cosas tontas.

– ¿Cómo pueden ser así? ¿Cómo pueden abandonar a su hija? ¿¡Que acaso no les importa!?– Grité.

Su padre se acercó a mí y me tomo del cuello, no apretaba, no tenía fuerzas para hacerlo, me miraba con el rostro lleno de lágrimas, estaba sufriendo mucho.

– ¡Todo esto es tu culpa! Tuvo la idea de volver a aquella ciudad, la apoyamos, pensamos que sería lo mejor para ella… entonces simplemente desfalleció, ¡cayo frente a nuestros ojos! Y desde entonces… ella esta así… desde hace un año. –

Mi culpa… todo fue mi culpa, eso decían ellos, aunque claramente solo estaban frustrados, su madre no dejaba de llorar, era a la que más le dolía, comenzaban a culpar a cualquiera, cuando fuese como fuese, esto hubiese pasado, pero no podía dejar de sentirme mal. Nunca… nunca le di una respuesta y ahora ella… se iba a ir más lejos de mí. Empuje a su padre y a su madre, cubrí a María con mis brazos.

– ¡No! ¡No la volverán a alejar de mí! Aléjese doctor, no le hará nada, ¡ella volverá! Yo lo se… porque me lo prometió. – Grite.

Llamaron por ayuda, me había aferrado a su cuerpo, no podían quitarme de ella, no quería dejarla irse más lejos, me dolía este adiós, entonces… lograron quitarme, me sostuvieron.

– ¡Déjenme malditos! ¡Aléjense de ella! – Grite con todas mis fuerzas. Comencé a patalear y tirar golpes, pero era inútil, me tenían bien controlado, mire como le ponían un fin a todo… llore y grite, pero ella no reacciono, sus padres solo apartaron la mirada y todo acabó.

Lo lograron, la alejaron de mi a un lugar en el cual no podía alcanzarla, mire al cielo y le pedí a dios que me la devolviera, que la trajera nuevamente conmigo, que había cosas que no le había dicho, no podía dejar de rasgarme el rostro de la frustración y llorar más fuerte. Me tiré al suelo, no podía estar siquiera de pie, no quería seguir en dicho lugar, no pude cambiar nada, no pude ayudarla. Cerré mis ojos y tape mis oídos, no quería ver ni oír más, pasé unos minutos en llanto hasta que perdí el conocimiento, entonces... desperté.

Abrí los ojos y un pequeño rostro me miraba. Una niña de piel blanca y ojos verdes como esmeraldas estaba frente a mi... era María, pero no la que conocía, era una niña nuevamente.

– Estabas llorando – Me dijo.

Me estaba abrazando, no entendía nada.

– Pero tu... moriste, yo lo miré, no pude hacer nada al final. – Dije.

– Pero si solo estaba durmiendo. –

Entonces lo comprendí, era nuevamente un niño, volví a aquel día cuando ella durmió por primera vez.

– Todo estará bien – Me dijo mientras me acariciaba la cabeza. – solo fue una pesadilla–

Era verdad, solo había sido una pesadilla, ella nunca se apartó de mí.

Así que antes de que algo pasara, la abrace con todas mis fuerzas.

– No te alejes más de mil por favor, hay lugares a los que no puedo ir, no quiero perderte nuevamente. –

Me miro y sonrió.

– No iré a ningún lado – Me dijo.

"Porque yo... quiero pasar el resto de mi vida contigo."

Historia #3: Ella siempre me supera.

Conozco a una chica desde pequeños; al ser mi vecina nos criamos prácticamente juntos. Todos los días jugábamos juntos.

¿Cómo llegué a tener una relación de amistad con ella? Pues la respuesta es simple.

– ¡Se mi amigo! – Gritó enfrente de mí.

No la conocía para ese entonces, era la primera vez que nos mirábamos. Tenía alrededor de unos seis años. Solamente conocía que ella era mi vecina, pero nada más allá de eso.

Por supuesto no supe cómo responder a su pedido; uno no simplemente se lanza y le pide a otra persona que formen una amistad. En lo absoluto. Era vergonzoso, pero ella… ¡Sonreía! Sonreía con una gracia que se contagiaba.

A la pura vista se podía notar que ella era una de esas chicas energéticas que siempre está feliz y jugando. Yo por otro lado era… un poco más apático. No era como si me desagradara, como dije antes, no la conocía. Simplemente… no sentía la misma emoción que ella.

– ¿Por qué? – Le pregunté sin pensarlo.

No buscaba ser grosero o alejarla, solo… me interesaba saber el por qué me buscaba a mí en específico.

– No hay más niños en esta calle. – Me respondió sin perder su sonrisa. – Y parece que también quieres divertirte, así que juguemos.

–

Ciertamente no tenía amigos en aquel entonces, y no era un problema. Aun no comenzaba a ir a la escuela, y como ella lo había dicho, no había más niños en esa calle. Pero aun así… la idea de jugar junto a una niña… usualmente no era lo común.

– No creo que quieras jugar conmigo. – Le respondí. – Yo no juego con muñecas como tú, tampoco a la casita o cosas así. –

– ¡Yo tampoco! – Respondió.

Me tomó de la mano y me estiró con fuerza.

– Juaguemos a las escondidas. – Me dijo. – Esta vez yo cuento, anda a esconderte. –

Era como si ignorara todos los peros que pusiera y tomara únicamente las partes donde yo aceptaba, las cuales no eran ninguna.

Se puso en la pared y comenzó a contar. Para ese momento una idea pasó por mi cabeza: "Vuelve a casa" Nadie me podía obligar a estar ahí con ella, bueno, quizá mamá o papá lo hubieran hecho, pero ellos no estaban ahí. Podía simplemente abandonarla en lo que ella contaba y volver a la comodidad de casa. Pero…

Terminé escondiéndome no muy lejos de ahí. Sentí que volver a casa no era lo correcto, aun si solo era un niño egoísta, tenía un corazón y una conciencia, la cual me estaría matando por dejarla ahí después de estar tan animada respecto al jugar.

Pasaron los minutos, cada vez se hacia mas tarde. Ella no me encontraba, me comencé a preguntar si era que me había escondido muy bien… o quizá ella se aburrió. Si me dejó ahí. No hubiera sido extraño, después de todo, yo me había negado muchas veces y quizá eso la cansó. Pensé que quizá lo hacia para darme una lección.

Pero entonces, miré nuevamente su rostro.

– ¡Te encontré! – Gritó llena de alegría.

Sentí como si esas palabras tuvieran mas de un significado. No solo me había encontrado de mi escondite, sino…

Algo movió mi corazón, y por primera vez en mucho tiempo, pude sonreír también de felicidad.

Nuestra amistad de afinó con el tiempo. Resultó que terminamos en la misma escuela primaria, en la misma aula, y sentados uno al lado del otro.

Aquello hizo llevadera la escuela, ella siempre hacia algo entretenido o me contaba cosas extrañas. Regularmente la regañaban por no callarse en clase. Pero aun así volvía a contarme más y más cosas.

Secundaria también estuvimos juntos; éramos inseparables. Al lugar que ella fuera, yo también estaba ahí.

Seguía siendo mi vecina, por lo que frecuentaba mucho mi casa. Mi madre la adoraba, y mi padre daba indirectas de que yo ya estaba creciendo y que estaba orgulloso de mi.

Muchos de los comentarios los ignoraba. Lo único que hacíamos era… jugar en mi habitación, mirar películas, leer algunos comics; se convirtió en mi mejor amigo.

Aquello no duró mucho. Las cosas comenzaron a cambiar, y ella lo notó. Muchos hablaban de nosotros a las espaldas. De que era extraña la relación que llevábamos, que no estaban del todo seguros si un hombre y una mujer se podían llevar tan bien. Y ella dio el siguiente paso.

– Prácticamente ya lo somos, ¿no? – Me preguntó energética como siempre.

– ¿A que te refieres? – Le pregunté.

– ¡Somos pareja! – Respondió tomando la delantera.

– ¿¡Lo somos!? – Aquello me sorprendió.

Pero viendo la relación que llevábamos, era comprensible. Todos a nuestro alrededor lo pensaban igual. Entonces… solo debíamos hacerlo "Formal". Ella no me desagradaba en lo absoluto, disfrutaba estar con ella todo el tiempo. Me entendía mejor que nadie más, y creía yo también lo hacía.

Una vez más… me superó. Tomó las riendas y dijo lo que yo no hubiera podido decir.

– ¿Algo cambiara? – Le pregunté.

Nunca tuvimos una pareja, por lo que no comprendíamos que era serlo.

– No lo creo. – Respondió alegre. – Solo que así puedo decir felizmente que te quiero. –

Decía las cosas mas vergonzosas sin pensárselo. Pero eso no me desagradaba.

Llegamos a preparatoria. Nuevamente fuimos a la misma. Seguíamos siendo pareja de lo mas normal. Bueno, quizá no tan normal. Parecíamos hermanos o amigos por como nos comportábamos. Pero no había otra forma de hacerlo, siempre estuvo a mi lado, la confianza estaba a otro nivel. Bromear con ella de cualquier cosa era el pan de cada día.

Elegimos la misma universidad, la misma carrera. A ambos nos gustaban las mismas cosas, queríamos estudiar lo mismo y trabajar juntos en los proyectos que teníamos a futuro.

Lo que me llevó a pensar que quizá… me faltaba dar un paso mas allá. Ella dio los primeros dos; ella forjó nuestra amistad, ella inicio nuestra relación. Y al pensar en mi futuro, ella siempre estaba ahí. Yo… quería ser el que diera el siguiente paso.

El día de la graduación llegó. Nos graduamos con honores, éramos el equipo dinamita. Nada nos podía detener.

Era hora de comenzar la vida adulta. Y aun ella no daba el siguiente paso. Quizá… ella no lo quería dar. Comencé a dudar, aun si yo quería darlo, quizá ella en realidad no. Quizá estaba aburrida de nuestra relación y quería terminarlo.

Pero por mas que intentaba mirar un futuro sin ella… me era imposible. La conocí desde pequeña y nunca se apartó de mi lado. Quería decírselo, que quería nuestra vida nunca se separara. Aun si ella no lo miraba de la misma forma… no quería guardar esos sentimientos.

– Yo… quería pedirte algo. – Le dije.

– ¿Qué podría ser? – Preguntó confundida.

Tome el valor que me faltaba. Era el momento. Esta vez yo… sería quien daría el siguiente paso, no quería que ella me superara una vez más.

– Lo he estado pensando durante un largo tiempo… quizá tu no sientes lo mismo, pero yo… en verdad lo quiero. – Dije. – Han sido unos largos años, y no los cambiaria para nada. Has alegrado mi vida de una forma que no te puedes imaginar, y por lo mismo… quiero que estés en todo lo que esta por venir. Por favor… ¡CASATE

CONMIGO! –

Con una expresión de sorpresa, quedó en silencio.

Pensé que quizá, después de todo, ella no…

– ¿No lo estábamos ya? – Preguntó confundida.

– ¿Eh? – No comprendí su respuesta.

– Me adelante un poco y rente un departamento. – Me dijo. – ¡Por supuesto que yo también quiero que estés en mi futuro! –

¿Un departamento? Ella… yo… no pude aguantar las lagrimas de felicidad.

Una vez más… ella… me superó.

– Me alegro de haberte encontrado… –

26183883R00118

Printed in Great Britain
by Amazon